NICHOLAS WRIGHT

Nicholas Wright's plays include V   .er
Award for Best New Play, 2003) an   production of
Mrs Klein, at the National Theatre, ii   st End and in New
York; *Treetops* and *One Fine Day* at Riverside Studios; *The Gorky Brigade* at the Royal Court; *The Crimes of Vautrin* for Joint Stock; *The Custom of the Country* and *The Desert Air* for the RSC; *Cressida* for the Almeida and *The Reporter* at the National. Adaptations include *His Dark Materials*, *Three Sisters* and *John Gabriel Borkman* for the National; *Thérèse Raquin* at Chichester Festival Theatre and the National; and *Naked* and *Lulu* at the Almeida, where *Mrs Klein* was also revived in 2009. He wrote the ballet scenario for Christopher Wheeldon's *Alice's Adventures in Wonderland* for the Royal Ballet, the libretti for Rachel Portman's opera *The Little Prince* (Houston Grand Opera) and for Jonathan Dove's opera for television, *Man on the Moon*, based on the Apollo 11 Moon landing. Other writing for television includes adaptations of *More Tales of the City* and *The No. 1 Ladies' Detective Agency* (BBC/HBO). His writing about the theatre includes *99 Plays*, a personal view of playwriting from Aeschylus to the present day, and *Changing Stages: A View of British Theatre in the Twentieth Century*, co-written with Richard Eyre.

Other Titles in this Series

RATTIGAN'S NIJINSKY

Nicholas Wright

based on the screenplay by
Terence Rattigan

NICK HERN BOOKS
London
www.nickhernbooks.co.uk

A Nick Hern Book

Rattigan's Nijinsky first published in 2011 by Nick Hern Books
Limited, 14 Larden Road, London W3 7ST

Rattigan's Nijinsky copyright © 2011 Nicholas Wright and the Trustess
of the Sir Terence Rattigan Charitable Trust

Nicholas Wright has asserted his right to be identified as the author of
this work

Cover image: SWD (www.swd.uk.com)
Cover design: Ned Hoste, 2H

Typeset by Nick Hern Books, London
Printed in the UK by CLE Print Ltd, St Ives, Cambs PE27 3LE

A CIP catalogue record for this book is available from the British Library

ISBN 978 1 84842 167 7

FSC
www.fsc.org
MIX
From responsible
sources
FSC® C019549

Introduction

Philip Franks rang me unexpectedly in September 2010 to ask if I'd be interested in adapting a Rattigan screenplay about Nijinsky. The usual form is for playwrights to be grandly equivocal when requests like this are made: 'Mmm... I'll need a few days to think about it.' So my reply must have startled him. I had huge admiration for Terence Rattigan, I said, I'd been researching a play about Diaghilev's company, the Ballets Russes, for years, though I hadn't yet written a word of it, I loved classical dance and I was at that moment working with Christopher Wheeldon on a full-length *Alice* for the Royal Ballet. When could I start? We met and he gave me the script.

As Philip had warned me, it wasn't performable onstage: there were too many short, choppy scenes, crowded set-pieces, mandatory close-ups, packed auditoria, train rides and an enormous cast. In common with most good screenplays, the dialogue was sparse. But on its own terms it was excellent.

The history of the Nijinsky/Diaghilev relationship, and of the Ballets Russes is a complex one. As always happens when people realise that what they're creating is radically new, practically everyone involved felt compelled to write about it, and those who didn't became the subject of scholarly biographies. Add to these a welter of programmes, newspaper announcements and reviews, and there cannot have been a minute in the life of Diaghilev's company that hasn't been documented somewhere or other. Rattigan's brilliance was to fillet this mass of material down to a lucid and moving story about a love affair that was an emotional disaster but an artistic triumph.

I searched the script for clues to why he had written it. He must have known that an Edward Albee-scripted Nijinsky movie project, starring Nureyev and Paul Scofield, had recently had the plugs pulled on it by the producer, Harry Saltzman, and the commercial potential can't have escaped him. But he must also have realised that he would be doing something very untypical: he would be writing an explicitly homosexual play. Did the knowledge that he hadn't long to live fuel the desire, finally, to write about his own sexuality? There's support for this in an exquisite long scene that breathes experience: one gay lover tries to end the relationship as kindly as he can, while the other one closes the door on the painfulness of it all. Behind it lies the dour conviction that love can never be equal: one lover will always be more loved than the other.

He had many links with ballet. Years before, he had had a lover who was a ballet dancer, before becoming a successful TV director: Adrian Brown, who talked eloquently to me about their relationship. Rattigan had placed a male dancer at the centre of his unsuccessful *Variation on a Theme*, and in 1968 he had set his unperformed ('In fact, unread') music/dance/drama event *Pas de Deux* in the world of ballet. Both Frederick Ashton and the choreographer and director William Chappell were close friends, and they must surely take some credit for the screenplay's technical accuracy.

And Diaghilev had cropped up in his life before. In an anonymous squib entitled *Drama v. Binkie*, he had examined, in the form of a mock trial, the record of Binkie Beaumont, the canny, gay and rigidly conservative producer who exercised iron control over the West End theatre, and who had produced a number of Rattigan's plays. 'Compared to the great impresarios of the past, such as Sir Charles Cochran or Diaghilev, Binkie is guilty,' Rattigan had written. 'Binkie's talent is as a manager of genius but the theatre stands in urgent need not of a manager but of an impresario.' Was Rattigan rattling the bars of the gilded cage in which Binkie had locked him? Did he long for a producer who could inspire him in a way that Binkie never had? Was the long-dead Diaghilev his imagined answer?

There's a curiosity about the script. I'm looking at a copy now. It was printed by a company called Odanti, who printed everyone's plays in the days before computers were invented, and it looks like any other conventional script. But if you open it, you'll find that at odd occasions, and in the most unusual way, a stage direction explodes in a riff of anger and frustration. Why are 'great first nights' always filmed so badly, he asks? Why, after his 'long and turbulent career', do people persist in thinking they know more about writing plays than he does? I've included a couple of these in the play: they're too revealing to leave out.

But how to stage the unstageable? A couple of paragraphs in Michael Darlow's biography of Rattigan gave a clue. *Nijinsky* was commissioned by the BBC in 1972, as a potential 'Play of the Month'. But when Romola, Nijinsky's widow, got wind of the project she opposed it furiously. Legally speaking, she had no case, but her threats were so alarming to Rattigan that he persuaded the BBC not to produce the play during her lifetime. As he must have known, postponed projects never get made for the simple reason that everyone loses interest in them. *Nijinsky* was never produced. As Michael Darlow puts it, 'Rattigan regretted this for the rest of his life.'

This seemed the perfect springboard for what Philip and I thought of as a 'meta-play' – one that not only provided the frame for a fine but unknown Rattigan creation, but saw *through* the picture, as it were, to give an impression of the man who wrote it, why he wrote it, what it meant to him and why he suppressed it. It was also a welcome opportunity to create a portrait, not of the smiling, imperturbable Rattigan of legend, but of a writer beset by his sense of failure, mortally ill and coursing towards a messy and angry death – just as the suave surfaces of his plays conceal disorderly passions.

Philip and I visited Michael Darlow, who told us about the interviews that he and Gillian Hodson had carried out with Rattigan in 1977... interviews interrupted while Rattigan dosed himself with his painkiller button or poured a drink from the dozen bottles of brandy stacked on the hospital floor. Other routes of research turned out to be blind alleys. I had hoped to find Romola's acrimonious correspondence in the British Library's Rattigan collection, but there was no sign of it at all, nor of anything that gave even a flavour of the *Nijinsky* affair. The normally capacious BBC Archive had nothing either, nor did Rattigan's agent, nor did the files of Rattigan's lawyer, Peter

Carter-Ruck. When I reported back to Philip on the absence of evidence and the empty boxes, he remarked, 'This is getting more and more like a Margery Allingham thriller.' I had a long talk, just before Christmas, with Alan Shallcross, a delightful man who had been script editor on 'Play of the Month' and who assured me over the phone that, if I travelled up to see him in North Yorkshire, he'd tell me everything he could recall. But he died before I could get to see him.

Despite the failure of my amateur detective work, the play was a joy to write. So well-honed and craftsmanlike was Rattigan's storytelling that my contribution seemed to write itself. He had done the heavy lifting, now I was having the fun. The idea that the two plays might merge, like whirls of atoms sharing the same space, came very naturally. (As it turned out, the resulting play is written by Rattigan and Wright in roughly equal parts.) Philip suggested to me that Terry and Romola might meet, along the lines of the imaginary meeting between Mary Stuart and Elizabeth I in Schiller's *Mary Stuart*, and I saw the value of this at once. I'd never met Rattigan (I was much too nervous), but two friends of mine, the director Frith Banbury and the actor Robert Flemyng, both dead now, had known him well, or as well as anyone did, and their memories of him came back to me as vividly and as waspishly as ever, and many have gone into the play.

Cedric Messina has been a resonant name for me ever since, as a small boy in Cape Town, I would stay awake late at night listening to his prestige drama productions on a radio hidden under the eiderdown. He was a maverick at the BBC: a South African, not Oxbridge but a self-made showman. He died in 1993. Rattigan died, after many rallies and setbacks, in 1977. Romola nursed her husband for the rest of his life; he died in London in 1950 at the age of sixty, still deranged and almost incapable of speech. Karsavina retired to London, advised at the Royal Ballet from time to time and died at the age of ninety-three. Diaghilev continued to heed the fortune-teller's warning, never venturing on a ship unless it was essential. In 1929, gravely ill, he went to Venice where he died, as prophesied, on water.

Nicholas Wright, 2011

Thanks

Great thanks are due from me to Alan Brodie – the representative of the Terence Rattigan Trust – for his suggestion of the original screenplay and, both to him and the Trust itself, for permission to adapt it. Thanks to Michael Darlow and Adrian Brown, for the help that I've described. Finally, grateful thanks to Gergely and Irina Stewart for Russian and Hungarian translation and to John Sackville-West for cricketing know-how.

N.W.

Rattigan's Nijinsky was first performed at the Chichester
Festival Theatre on 19 July 2011, with the following cast:

ROMOLA DE PULZKY	Faye Castelow
GEORGES ASTRUC / OTTO KHAN / PROFESSOR BLEULER	Pip Donaghy
DONALD / VASLAV NIJINSKY	Joseph Drake
ELEANORA NIJINSKY / TAMARA KARSAVINA	Emma Harris
NICOLAI LEGAT / BARON DE GUNSBERG / DR FRENKEL	John Hopkins
SERGEI DIAGHILEV / CEDRIC MESSINA	Jonathan Hyde
LEONID MASSINE / ALEXANDRE BENOIS / SHIP'S PURSER	Louis Maskell
ANNA	Ellie Robertson
TERENCE RATTIGAN	Malcolm Sinclair
OLD ROMOLA / VERA RATTIGAN / EMILIA MARKUS	Susan Tracy
EXAMINER / LEON BAKST / VASLAV GRIGORIEV / ADOLF BOLM	Ewan Wardop

Other parts played by members of the company

Director	Philip Franks
Designer	Mike Britton
Lighting Designer	Johanna Town
Music	Matthew Scott
Choreographer	Quinny Sacks

Characters

TERENCE RATTIGAN (TERRY)
DONALD, *a roomboy*
BALLET SCHOOL EXAMINER
ELEANORA NIJINSKY, *Nijinsky's mother*
YOUNG VASLAV NIJINSKY
NICOLAI LEGAT, *ballet-master*
SERGEI DIAGHILEV, *impresario*
GEORGES ASTRUC, *Parisian impresario*
LEON BAKST, *stage designer*
ALEXANDRE BENOIS, *stage designer*
TAMARA KARSAVINA, *dancer*
VASLAV NIJINSKY, *dancer*
VASLAV GRIGORIEV, *company manager*
ROMOLA DE PULZKY, *later Romola Nijinsky*
OLD ROMOLA NIJINSKY
VERA RATTIGAN, *Terry's mother*
ANNA, *Romola's maid*
SHIP'S PURSER
ADOLPH BOLM, *dancer*
BARON DE GUNZBURG, *theatre backer*
CEDRIC MESSINA, *BBC drama producer*
EMILIA MARKUS, *actress, Romola's mother*
LEONID MASSINE, *dancer*
OTTO KAHN, *New York impresario*
DR FRENKEL
PROFESSOR BLEULER, *psychologist*

Plus porters, hotel staff, aspirant ballet students, theatre attendants, dancers, reporters, lawyers, ship's stewards

Setting

Time: 1974 and earlier

Place: A suite in Claridge's Hotel, London, and other places

This text went to press before the end of rehearsals, and so may differ slightly from the play as performed.

ACT ONE

1974. The living room of a top-of-the-range, two-room suite in Claridge's Hotel. Two doors, one to the hall, one to the bedroom. But they can change identity when needed.

A CHAMBERMAID *comes in carrying towels. She turns on the radio, listens to a few bars of a pop song of the period and takes the towels through to the bedroom next door, en route to the bathroom, dancing a few disco steps.*

As she goes, a line of HOTEL STAFF *enters from outside, uniformed in classic manner. Some carry expensive luggage through to the bedroom, others turn on lights and turn off the radio.*

TERENCE RATTIGAN (TERRY) *follows them in. He is sixty-three, immaculately dressed and groomed but plainly ill. A roomboy,* DONALD, *hovers with a briefcase.*

TERRY. Yes, give me that.

    DONALD *does so, then busies himself around the room, plumping cushions, laying out the hotel stationery, etc.* TERRY *opens the briefcase, takes out a clinical-looking bottle. Finds a script, glances at it and puts it somewhere.*

    The HOTEL STAFF *come out of the bedroom.* TERRY *tips the senior* PORTER *a tenner.*

That will be all.

PORTER. Thank you, Sir Terence. Have a good evening.

TERRY. I'll do my best.

    TERRY *goes out to the bedroom en route to the toilet. The* HOTEL STAFF *leave, except for* DONALD *and the* CHAMBERMAID, *who linger.* DONALD *reads silently from the script, then laughs quietly.*

CHAMBERMAID. What?

DONALD (*reading*). '*Nijinsky*, a screenplay.'

He turns a page.

'We find ourselves, on the 20th of August, 1898, in a large room at the Imperial School of Ballet in St Petersburg, where as many small boys as can be afforded are preparing for their auditions for the Mariinsky Theatre, combing their hair or trying out their immature arabesques...'

TERRY *appears in the doorway.*

TERRY. Put that down!

DONALD *does, and the* CHAMBERMAID *makes herself scarce.*

DONALD. I'm sorry, sir.

TERRY. It's private. What are you waiting for?

DONALD. In case there's anything else you wanted, sir.

TERRY. Well, no, there isn't.

DONALD *turns to go.*

Oh, hang on.

He takes a tenner out of his wallet.

Can you bring me up a bottle of J&B? You do have J&B? You always used to.

DONALD. I expect we do, sir. It's just that it isn't that often asked for.

TERRY. Well, do what you can. Or Haig will do.

DONALD *goes.* TERRY *sits.*

(*Murmurs.*) Damn cheek.

He lights a cigarette, glances at the screenplay, turns it over and dials the number that he's written on the back. There's an answer.

Is that the BBC? I want the 'Play of the Month' department.
(*Pause*.) Yes, obviously it's drama. (*Pause*.) I'll wait.

*He coughs and the cough awakens a pain in a shoulder
blade. He puts his hand over it, rubs it. The call is answered.*

Hello, yes. Can I speak to Cedric Messina. Tell him it's
Terry. Terence Rattigan.

The pain gets worse.

Shit.

*He takes a swig from the clinical bottle. The call is
answered.*

Oh, Cedric. Yes, I'm back and I'm totally fine. (*Pause*.) No,
really I am. One of my doctors in Bermuda turned out to be an
ardent theatre fan, so he's given me this marvellous new
painkilling... *sludge* that one's not really supposed to be
taking. (*Pause*.) No, I'm perfectly lucid, thank you. And this
will amuse you... he's been pumping me full of hormones.
(*Pause*.) No, the other kind, sadly. *Anti*-male. (*Pause*.) Cedric,
that's a very indelicate question and the answer is no, I can't.
(*Pause*.) Of course I miss it, wouldn't you? No other side
effects. I suppose there could be. I might start writing like
Dodie Smith. But look, I've not just rung for a chat. It's about
the widow. (*Pause*.) Well, will you call me as soon as you can?
It's quite important. (*Pause*.) Claridge's. Room number...

The key is out of reach.

... I don't remember, you'll just have to ask for me.

Rings off. Rubs his shoulder blade. Takes another swig.

Come *on*.

*He stands waiting until, after a few moments, to the
accompaniment of a calming strain of music, the pain
dissolves.*

The room looks different: it's the quality of light. TERRY
*stays where he is, looking round and taking in the changed
atmosphere. Turning around, he sees that a small boy has*

*appeared, standing on one leg and attempting an arabesque.
Now another appears from somewhere else... and then as
many as can be afforded, swarming out from behind the
furniture, from under the desk, etc., and finding a clear spot
to perform their ballet exercises. One boy stands apart,
biting his thumb: this is the* YOUNG VASLAV NIJINSKY,
accompanied by his mother, ELEANORA NIJINSKY.

TERRY *watches, only slightly bewildered. A* BALLET
SCHOOL EXAMINER, *with lists and files, appears.*

EXAMINER. May I have silence, please!

The BOYS *settle down, while the* EXAMINER *turns his
attention to a* LIKELY LAD *who is being examined.*

And lastly, young man, why do you want to be a dancer?

LIKELY LAD. Because I believe that it's the best way in which
I can serve my country and the Tsar.

EXAMINER. An admirable reply. Go and wait with the others.

(*Addressing the room.*) Boys and parents! I am sorry to tell
you this, but this year there are no fewer than one hundred
and sixty-three candidates for the Tsar's Imperial Ballet
School...

The BOYS *utter impressed 'whoos' at this number.*

... while we are empowered to take only five new students. I
repeat, only five, because of the reductions in the latest
Imperial budget for the arts.

Groans.

We have petitioned our noble patron, the Grand Duke
Nicholas, but to no avail. I am sorry. Very sorry. But it is not
my fault.

He consults a list.

Now that I have concluded the verbal examinations, you are
all required to proceed to the adjacent room... through
there... and await your turn for the physical tests.

The BOYS *are about to do so, but…*

ELEANORA. But you haven't seen my son!

EXAMINER. Your son, Madame?

He looks at his list.

(*Reads.*) 'Vaslav Nijinsky.' Is this the boy?

VASLAV *holds back, still biting his thumb.*

Step forward.

ELEANORA *makes the sign of the cross and pushes him
forward.*

ELEANORA. Go, Vaslav. Go with God.

VASLAV. But, Mother…

ELEANORA. Go!

He stands before the EXAMINER, *who looks doubtfully at
him. The other* BOYS *watch, amused by* VASLAV *as though
by a halfwit.*

EXAMINER. How old are you?

VASLAV. Nine.

EXAMINER. Nine years old? You're very small. Are you
telling the truth? Give me your papers.

Pause.

Your *papers.*

VASLAV *produces them, then drops them on the floor.
Annoyed, the* EXAMINER *picks the papers up.*

(*Reads.*) Born 1889… Ah, a Pole… that explains it.

He glances contemptuously at the boy.

Typically underdeveloped. Now, Master… Nijinsky, are you
ready for a question?

VASLAV *nods.*

If your mother gave you ten roubles to buy four strawberry cakes costing thirty-five kopecks each... how much change would you give her on your return?

Pause.

VASLAV. None.

EXAMINER. Why none?

VASLAV. Because if any money was left over, I'd have spent it.

EXAMINER. But how much would you have left over?

VASLAV. I think... enough to buy me a paintbox.

EXAMINER. How much does a paintbox cost?

VASLAV. I don't know. Anyway, my mother doesn't like strawberry cakes. And she doesn't want me to have another paintbox. So the question is silly, isn't it?

The EXAMINER *lays down his pen, having given up the case as hopeless.*

EXAMINER. Do you have to nibble your thumb?

VASLAV thinks this is the first sensible question he's been asked.

VASLAV. Yes!

EXAMINER. Why?

VASLAV. I don't know. The doctor says it's a sign of mental disturbance.

The EXAMINER *makes a heavy note.*

EXAMINER. Is there much mental illness in your family?

VASLAV. Yes, quite a lot. My father is often mad, and my brother Stanislav is in an asylum.

The other BOYS *laugh uproariously.*

EXAMINER. How very tragic. May I ask you why your mother won't let you have another paintbox? Is it because you suck the brushes?

VASLAV. Yes.

EXAMINER. With the paint still on them?

VASLAV. How did you guess?

EXAMINER. I have second sight.

The other BOYS *laugh at this witticism while the* EXAMINER *makes a quick note.*

I'm sorry to tell you, Master Nijinsky, that you are four inches under the regulation height. When you are fully grown, you will still be far too short to be a ballet dancer. You needn't waste your time on the physical examination. There's no future for you here.

A flicker of incomprehension crosses VASLAV*'s face. It turns to fury and he grabs the* EXAMINER*'s arm.*

VASLAV. No *future*?

NICOLAI LEGAT, *the ballet-master, enters. He carries a slender ballet stick. The* EXAMINER *removes his arm from* VASLAV*'s grip.*

LEGAT. Do we have trouble with this boy?

The other BOYS *compete with each other to point out what a disaster* VASLAV *has been so far: 'Yes, sir! Yes, sir!' But:*

EXAMINER. Silence! This is Maître Legat, the ballet-master.

(*To* LEGAT.) See for yourself, Nikolai Gustavovich.

He passes LEGAT *his notes.* VASLAV, *meanwhile, withdraws to a corner, where he crouches, staring with deadly venom at the two adults.*

And just look at his school reports.

LEGAT *scans the documents then hands them back.*

LEGAT. Deplorable.

(*To* VASLAV.) Is your father Thomas Nijinsky?

ELEANORA. That is his father. He's my husband.

LEGAT (*to the* EXAMINER). A very fine dancer. With a remarkable leap.

(*To* VASLAV.) Stand up.

There is no response.

(*Sharply.*) I said, stand up!

VASLAV *stands.* LEGAT *walks around him, inspecting him with an analytical eye.* VASLAV *looks at him with suspicion. Suddenly* LEGAT *kneels and feels the boy's thigh.* VASLAV *tries to remove the hand. With casual violence,* LEGAT *knocks the boy's hand away. He stands.*

I want you to jump over this, from a standing position.

He holds out his ballet stick about two feet from the ground. VASLAV *glares.*

Jump! Yes, *now!*

VASLAV *shrugs, raises* LEGAT*'s stick to roughly double its height. Then, from a standing position,* VASLAV *leaps high over the stick.*

The moment is broken by the ringing of the telephone. TERRY *answers it as the* BOYS, ELEANORA, LEGAT *and the* EXAMINER *go into the adjacent room.*

TERRY (*into phone*). Cedric, hello. (*Pause.*) Don't worry, I've been quite happy waiting. I simply wanted to… (*Pause.*) That's right, to check the legal situation with you. What do *your* lawyers think? The BBC does *have* a legal department, doesn't it?

He stops as one of the doors opens and a line of HOTEL STAFF *comes in, an echo of the previous one, carrying luggage through to the adjacent room.*

Hello?

A PORTER *holds the door open for* SERGEI DIAGHILEV.

PORTER. Monsieur Diaghilev.

DIAGHILEV *comes in and glances at* TERRY.

TERRY. *Hello?*

(*Into phone.*) No, there's nobody here. No, I haven't, not a drop, not since the plane. I've sent a cherub for a bottle of J&B, does that count against me? Cedric, will you shut up and listen? I'm meeting the widow here at five o'clock.

DIAGHILEV. Whose widow is this?

TERRY (*to* DIAGHILEV). Nijinsky's.

DIAGHILEV. You mean Romola?

TERRY. Romola, yes, exactly. (*Into phone.*) Yes, I *know* you know. Now, I've read all the stuff from Carter-Ruck, and as far as I can understand the legal gobbledegook, it doesn't matter *what* she thinks about the screenplay because she hasn't a leg to stand on. So I can tell her to take a flying fuck at a rolling doughnut, is that correct? (*Pause.*) Yes, of course I'll say it nicely. I don't make a habit of giving heart attacks to eighty-year-old ladies. So when can we meet? (*Pause.*) No, I'll be at Lord's all day watching England playing India. Pop in this evening. (*Pause.*) Later. *Later.*

He rings off. The HOTEL STAFF *have gone.*

DIAGHILEV. Romola is a monster.

TERRY. I'm used to monsters. I've been having my plays done in the West End for forty years.

DIAGHILEV. She had the naked effrontery to write in her book that it was *I* who seduced *Nijinsky.*

TERRY. You mean you didn't?

DIAGHILEV. Certainly not! I wasn't even attracted to him, not at first. The night that he came to see me, I thought he was just another complaining dancer.

A knock at the door.

Your roomboy.

It is indeed DONALD *with the whisky.*

DONALD. I've brought your J&B, Sir Terence.

TERRY. Thank you.

DONALD. Shall I pour it for you, sir?

TERRY. If you would.

> DONALD *pours him a whisky and* TERRY *takes the glass. He will continue drinking until he's finished the bottle, round about the end of the play, but he doesn't slur his words or slow down. His drunkenness is a heightened delusional state, more like cocaine than alcohol, aided by the morphine-based painkiller.*

DONALD. It's Donald, sir, if you need me again.

TERRY. Thank you. Donald. I shall remember that.

> DONALD *goes.*

DIAGHILEV. You can have that boy if you want. He made it perfectly clear.

TERRY. Don't be absurd. I'm ill.

DIAGHILEV. How ill?

TERRY. Well, put it like this. I would be well-advised to renew my membership of the MCC for a year, but two years would border on extravagance and three would be throwing my money away.

DIAGHILEV. But you're not distressed?

TERRY. I'm *very* distressed. But do you know what the English vice is? *Le vice Anglais?* It isn't spanking or hanging upside down from the chandeliers, or whatever the French imagine it to be. It's that we don't own up to our emotions. We think they demean us somehow.

> *Another knock at the door.*

DIAGHILEV. He's back.

> *The door opens revealing the actor who played* DONALD, *now as the nineteen-year-old* NIJINSKY. *We are in St Petersburg, 1909.*

NIJINSKY. Maître Diaghilev?

DIAGHILEV. Vaslav Nijinsky?

NIJINSKY *nods*.

Do you wish to speak with me?

NIJINSKY *nods*.

Is something the matter? Tell me!

NIJINSKY. May I come in?

DIAGHILEV. You may.

NIJINSKY *comes in*. DIAGHILEV *gestures towards a chair, and* NIJINSKY *sits*.

Are you dissatisfied with the roles that I have given you for the company's tour to Paris?

NIJINSKY. No, Maître.

DIAGHILEV. No, I could hardly imagine that you are. *Le Pavillon d'Armide*. *Le Festin*. *Les Sylphides*. You must have realised by now that Maestro Fokine considers you to be his muse?

NIJINSKY. I know that, Maître.

DIAGHILEV. You also know, I hope, that once the season in Paris is over, you will be free to return to the Mariinsky?

NIJINSKY *nods*.

So what do you want?

NIJINSKY. It's a delicate matter, Maître.

DIAGHILEV. So?

NIJINSKY. I've been rehearsing with your company for over a month, and no one has told me what I am going to be paid. I don't even know if I'm going to be paid at all. If it was only me, I would be happy to dance for the glory of God. But I have my mother to support.

DIAGHILEV *takes out a cigarette case, empties it and gives it to* NIJINSKY.

DIAGHILEV. Take it.

NIJINSKY *looks at it with care. Bites it.*

NIJINSKY. This is gold.

DIAGHILEV. I'd hardly give it away if it was worthless.

NIJINSKY. Thank you.

He kisses DIAGHILEV *fully. Pulls back.*

Have I embarrassed you?

DIAGHILEV. I'm... surprised. It was my impression that Prince Lvov was your protector.

NIJINSKY. That is the second thing I have to say.

DIAGHILEV. I'm listening?

NIJINSKY *bows formally.*

NIJINSKY. Prince Lvov presents his compliments, and suggests that I would be better off being protected by you.

DIAGHILEV. Because?

NIJINSKY. He says I don't have any conversation.

DIAGHILEV. I'd say you've packed in rather a lot so far.

NIJINSKY. But I don't know how to behave. I don't know which knife and fork to use, or how to eat an artichoke. The only French I know is ballet words like *bourrée* and *pas de chat.* I need a protector who will take the trouble to teach me to be a gentleman. Would you do that, Maître?

DIAGHILEV. I could try.

NIJINSKY. So shall we go to your bedroom?

DIAGHILEV. *Now?*

NIJINSKY *nods.* DIAGHILEV *goes to the bedroom door, opens it and* NIJINSKY *goes through. About to follow him,* DIAGHILEV *turns back to* TERRY.

I'm as powerless as a kitten when a boy says that he needs me.

TERRY. So am I.

DIAGHILEV. You too?

TERRY. Especially then.

> DIAGHILEV *closes the bedroom door and turns his attention to* TERRY.

DIAGHILEV. Do you like them small like him?

TERRY. I do. I doubt that I've ever had a lover over five foot eight and that would be pushing it.

DIAGHILEV. What else do you look for in a boy?

TERRY. Pretty is good. Polite is good. And preferably amusing.

DIAGHILEV. Do you look for talent?

TERRY (*dismissive*). No, no, no.

DIAGHILEV. So a genius wouldn't appeal to you?

TERRY. No, because a genius wouldn't need me.

DIAGHILEV. That's very good thinking! I should have thought of that myself. When Vaslav didn't need me any more, I went mad. It was as though my life didn't have any meaning. But that comes later. Where am I now?

TERRY. St Petersburg, 1909.

DIAGHILEV. That sounds correct.

> *The telephone rings.* DIAGHILEV *picks up the receiver and wipes it elaborately.* (*He always did this.*)

(*To* TERRY.) Germs.

(*Into phone.*) Operator, operator! This is too bad. You cut me off again. Now, I am not a man who exaggerates, but you have interrupted what is very likely the most important telephone call ever made from St Petersburg to Paris. After only a few minutes I find myself speaking to the air... Three hours, twenty-five minutes? For the nature of this telephone call, that *is* only a few minutes... to Monsieur Astruc, the great French impresario… Opera 22-34… as soon as possible, please… But of *course* it is on Imperial business.

(*To* TERRY.) Where are the others?

TERRY. The others?

DIAGHILEV. How could I be alone? I'm never alone. Grigoriev, my Chief of Staff, was at my side… Alexandre Benois, Leon Bakst…

TERRY. Don't worry about them. You're in close-up.

DIAGHILEV. I'm in *what*?

He turns his attention to the phone.

Hello? My dearest Astruc, I apologise for our atrocious telephone service… You rang off? But why? We had only just started… My dear fellow, I have no idea which of us is paying for the call. I discount such trivialities… Now, you interrupted me when I was dictating the form that your first advertisement should take in *Le Figaro*. It should be a whole page… Yes, that will cost some francs but I have wealthy friends who will see to that… you have my personal guarantee. Now, have you got pen and paper? Good. 'Monsieur Sergei Diaghilev, who astounded Paris last year with his season of Russian opera, is this year bringing to Paris the greatest ballet company ever assembled.' What is that extraordinary noise?

GEORGES ASTRUC *appears, on the telephone and eating a ham roll.*

ASTRUC. I am eating a sandwich.

DIAGHILEV. Could you eat it further away from the mouthpiece? It sounds like a Maxim gun. Where was I?

ASTRUC. Sergei Pavlovich, what is the point of all this? We know that since the Tsar removed your subsidy, you cannot possibly fulfil your side of the contract.

DIAGHILEV. Dear God, do I have to go into all that again? The money will be raised from other sources. I am even prepared to dig into my private capital.

ASTRUC. You haven't got any private capital.

DIAGHILEV. Now, is that the way to talk to an old friend? Leaving out my own ample resources, I have a thousand friends here who are clamouring to put their money into the historic season – the first ever visit of the Russian Ballet abroad. And the sets will be completed and paid for… Yes, by me! Leon Bakst is beside me at the moment, showing me the model for *Cléopatre*, and it's sublime.

LEON BAKST *appears around a door, carrying a beautiful model for* Cléopatre.

BAKST. You do realise there's no time to build it?

DIAGHILEV. Benois is assembling his model for *Pavillon d'Armide*.

ALEXANDRE BENOIS *appears carrying the model.*

BENOIS. Which you have just rejected, may God forgive you.

DIAGHILEV (*gently and paternally*). Quiet, children, please. I am talking to that dear, kind Monsieur Astruc, whom you all love.

BAKST *and* BENOIS *pull faces and* BENOIS *blows a raspberry.* DIAGHILEV*'s hand is over the receiver just in time. He removes it.*

They send you their deepest, most grateful love. So does little Tamara Karsavina…

(*Calls.*) Don't you, Tamara?

TAMARA KARSAVINA *appears in costume.*

KARSAVINA. Don't I what?

DIAGHILEV. Don't you send dear, kind, generous Monsieur Astruc your love?

KARSAVINA. I'll send him anything if he gets us to Paris, but if he's that silly little Frenchman you brought around at the Mariinsky, love is going just a little too far.

DIAGHILEV (*into the receiver*). A thousand adoring kisses. Now doesn't that make you feel better?

ASTRUC. No. Go on with your advertisement.

DIAGHILEV *puts his hand over the receiver.*

DIAGHILEV (*to the others*). I've got him.

All are delighted.

(*To* ASTRUC.) Ah, what a comfort it is to have you for a friend, my calm, cautious and very wise Gabriel! Now, Pavlova's name must appear no larger than that dear little Karsavina, who you have just been exchanging kisses with. Read out the names of the other dancers...

ASTRUC *wearily reads from a list.*

ASTRUC. Feodorova, Baldina, Smirnova. Men: Fokine, Monakov, Adolph Bolm...

DIAGHILEV. Bolm is a marvellous man, a beast, a savage!

ASTRUC. ... and then Nijinsky. Who is Nijinsky?

NIJINSKY *has come out of the bedroom, impeccably dressed in a new suit, gleaming shoes, tiepin.*

DIAGHILEV. *Who is Nijinsky?*

He stretches his hand out to take NIJINSKY*'s, which is not given but simply taken. No resistance, but no warmth or eagerness. The gesture is important.*

He is the greatest dancer in the world.

ASTRUC. But...

DIAGHILEV. I agree I haven't seen all the dancers in the world. While there is Nijinsky, I don't need to. He is the greatest dancer who ever lived, or who ever will live. Let me put it to you more simply – *entrechat-dix*.

ASTRUC (*unimpressed*). *Six?*

DIAGHILEV. *Six? Six?* Any *carthorse* can do *six*. I said *dix*. Has anyone ever done that before? He is going to be the greatest sensation of the age, and will make you a billion francs... Very well, and *merde* to you too, my beloved friend. Kisses shower on you from all my children – and from me.

He rings off, releases NIJINSKY*'s hand and gets up briskly.*

The battle has been won.

There is excited applause.

But may I remind you that the war is still to follow?

Paris. Sounds of a train and a busy station. Clouds of steam. HOTEL ATTENDANTS *and* ROOMBOYS *carry luggage across the stage and out.* ASTRUC *greets* DIAGHILEV, *who is dressed for travel in hat, furs and gloves. The two men embrace in a bear hug.*

ASTRUC. Welcome to Paris, my dear friend, welcome!

DIAGHILEV. Ah, Gabriel, my dearest Gabriel – what a joke I have for you! See? See? See?

Elaborately he pulls out the linings of all his pockets. Each one is empty. DIAGHILEV*'s roars of laughter grow louder, while* ASTRUC*'s polite titters become fainter, and finally end in the deadest of dead silences as the meaning of* DIAGHILEV*'s symbolic ritual strikes home.*

ASTRUC. You bring me nothing?

DIAGHILEV*'s laughter grows ever louder.*

DIAGHILEV. Not a single rouble...

He doubles up.

ASTRUC. Then there can be no season.

DIAGHILEV. I knew that's what you would say! Eh, how funny you are, my dear Gabriel! (*Growing serious.*) Now here is a list of my friends in Paris. Against each name, I have put the amount you will ask from them, and then the amount they will actually pay.

ASTRUC (*glances at it*). All these people lost money on your last season.

DIAGHILEV. So now you give them a chance to get it back.

ASTRUC. Sergei Pavlovich, it is quite impossible.

DIAGHILEV. Exactly. So it will be done. Why? Because it has to be done. Now...

He turns to NIJINSKY, *who is standing, patient and silent, in the background.*

... may I present Vaslav Nijinsky?

NIJINSKY *gives* ASTRUC *his formal bow and then his hand.*

ASTRUC. So you are the greatest dancer who ever lived?

NIJINSKY. Thanks be to God. I am.

The focus shrinks to a concentration on NIJINSKY. *He stands before a mirror – a hotel-room dressing table, let's say, or a full-length one, now doubling up as a mirror in* NIJINSKY's *dressing room at the Châtelet.*

NIJINSKY *studies himself intensely in the mirror.* DIAGHILEV *appears in a pool of light beside him.*

DIAGHILEV (*quietly, almost a whisper*). Tomorrow night, the 17th of May 1909, will be remembered... for as long as civilised art exists in the western world. You will enjoy a triumph the like of which has never been seen in modern times. On that, you have my personal guarantee.

DIAGHILEV *backs off into the darkness.* NIJINSKY *looks in the mirror, bites his thumb.*

NIJINSKY (*murmurs to his reflection*). Who are you? Are you Vaslav Nijinsky, the only man who has ever done *entrechat-dix*? (*Shakes his head.*) No, you are Armida's favourite slave – and also – you are a part of God – a part of Him – a part of Him.

(*Whispers.*) Oh God, let me be a part of You tonight.

He crosses himself and kneels. After a moment, he stands while other characters help him into his costume for Le Pavillon d'Armide.

Meanwhile:

DIAGHILEV (*addressing* TERRY). We are about to witness the most famous premiere in world history…

TERRY. … except that we're not going to see it…

DIAGHILEV (*dismayed*). … because…?

TERRY. … because that brilliant audience of famous men and women…

He picks up his screenplay and reads from it:

'… all of them dead except for Jean Cocteau, would rise from their graves in fury if I presented it, as so many, many "greatest theatrical triumphs of all time" have been presented in so many, many films – to wit by a small group of extras rising from their orchestra seats like rockets and applauding in a way that no audience has ever applauded: very, very fast, with their hands held very, very high above their heads. My feeling is that the *visual* should be replaced by the *aural*. For I have never heard, in either films or television, the sheer *volume* of sound with which a theatrical ovation can so excitingly split the ears.'

He throws down the script.

DIAGHILEV. So…

TERRY. … we're in the foyer of the Châtelet Theatre. Attendants are dozing in their chairs…

A couple of ATTENDANTS *doze in their chairs.*

… as they have dozed through so many other first nights. From behind the doors, we hear the finale rising to a climax. A younger attendant posted by one pair of doors, makes a signal and then, as the music ends, throws them open.

They do.

The other attendants wake…

They do.

… there is a moment's silence and suddenly the tumult erupts.

Applause is heard, then builds to immensity.

The camera shows the faces of the attendants as they begin to register surprise, then astonishment, then, frankly, disbelief.

FIRST ATTENDANT. But none of the audience have come out. Not even the critics!

SECOND ATTENDANT. What in the name of God is happening?

The effect is now of a reverse, as though the scene had revolved 180 degrees. We're now behind the tabs, witnessing a small, intensely concentrated group of DIAGHILEV, ASTRUC, KARSAVINA *and* NIJINSKY. ASTRUC *looks at his watch.*

ASTRUC (*to* DIAGHILEV). They won't go home, Sergei Pavlovich!

DIAGHILEV *looks at his watch.*

DIAGHILEV. I should hope not. They've only been applauding for half an hour.

Two FOOTMEN *draw the unseen curtains open.* NIJINSKY *and* KARSAVINA *step forward and bow.*

ASTRUC. This is the greatest triumph of all time!

DIAGHILEV. But of course, my dear Astruc. Didn't you have my personal guarantee? I think we should make an announcement tomorrow that we will give a few extra performances at, what do you think? Double the price?

ASTRUC (*aghast*). Double?

DIAGHILEV. We *could* get treble, but it is vulgar to be greedy. Perhaps between double and treble.

NIJINSKY *and* KARSAVINA *come back from their call,* KARSAVINA *holding her sides with laughter.*

KARSAVINA. An old lady... in the front row... threw Vaslav her diamond tiara.

DIAGHILEV. Where is it now?

NIJINSKY. It wasn't mine! I threw it back!

KARSAVINA. I saw it bounce across the stalls. He's *out of his mind*!

DIAGHILEV. Vaslav, we made history tonight. Let us make a little more. Be the first male dancer ever to take a solo call.

NIJINSKY. Oh, no... Sergei Pavlovich... no.

DIAGHILEV (*softly*). Do it, Vatzka. Do it for me.

NIJINSKY. You permit, Tamara?

KARSAVINA (*whom history records as an extremely nice and unaffected woman*). I insist.

Slowly, gracefully but still very shyly, as the noise increases, NIJINSKY *steps forward and performs his ritual bow.*

(*A contemporary description: 'He went quickly forward towards the footlights and, placing his right hand on his left shoulder, swept the arm down from left to right in a graceful gesture, at the same time inclining his head. His bearing was modest and dignified and his features were composed. It was a curious experience to contrast the quietly bowing figure onstage with the frenzied applause of the enraptured audience.'*)

We're back in TERRY*'s Claridge's suite.* TERRY *and* DIAGHILEV *are relaxed, drinking,* DIAGHILEV *smoking a cigar,* TERRY *smoking his usual cigarette. There's a clubbable atmosphere and you get the feeling that it's been like this for a while.*

DIAGHILEV. Of course... it could be...

TERRY.... yes...?

DIAGHILEV.... that Vaslav's insistence that his genius as a dancer came from God, excited a certain amount of envious irritation in me.

TERRY. I can imagine that it would.

DIAGHILEV. It was I who discovered the boy, I who educated him, I who presented him to the public with my characteristic flair. What did God have to do with it? But when I saw Nijinsky dance, it was quite clear to me that I could take no credit for that at all. It was, quite literally, divine. So I decided to make him a choreographer.

TERRY. Out of rivalry with God?

DIAGHILEV. To prove that, if He could create, then so could I.

TERRY. But can a choreographer be 'made'?

DIAGHILEV. I can make one whenever I want. I could make this ashtray into a choreographer. What I failed to see, was that my Vatzka would be just as great a genius *in that role*. That is what caused the catastrophe.

TERRY *drinks*.

TERRY. My own catastrophe came to a head on the first night of *Variation on a Theme*, with my darling Maggie Leighton in the lead. I'd spent the evening in a pub, and then I came back to watch the end of the show from the back of the stalls at the Globe. It seemed to have gone quite well. But there was something wrong with the applause. I didn't know what. A reticence. Nipped round to the dressing rooms, leaning against the corridor walls, suddenly realising how pissed I was. Maggie pushes me into the corner, says to me, 'Terry, was it really all right?' Her face is blurry through my drunkenness, but I could see the terror in her eyes. She says, 'I kept thinking that there was something about it that they didn't like.' I say, 'No, they were *gripped*, they were *absorbed*, that's why they were all so quiet.' Usual bollocks. Then it struck me. There *was* something they didn't like, and it was *me*. They were tired of me. There was something about my writing, or my playmaking or my style, that they *used* to like, that they liked quite a lot in fact, but now they'd had enough of it. And the ghastly thing was that I didn't know what it was. It wasn't as though I'd run out of tricks, because I don't *do* tricks. All I've got is the instinct for theatre that I've had since I was a schoolboy, and my instinct for what human beings are like. They're very simple instincts, they're childlike almost, and if they don't work any more, then I've got nothing left. I'm lost. I'm sunk. I knew all this standing in Maggie's dressing room, with the smell of her fabulous scent and the touch of her cheek and the buzzing about of the hangers-on and the popping of corks. I knew the party was over.

PORTERS *and* ROOMBOYS *enter with luggage and cross the stage. It's three years later. A hotel in Budapest. Schmaltzy Magyar violins play in the background.* DIAGHILEV, ASTRUC *and* VASLAV GRIGORIEV *are drinking champagne. The violins cross-fade with the sound, from behind a door, of Stravinsky banging out passages from 'The Rite of Spring' on a piano.*

DIAGHILEV. Budapest! City of muscular boys, cream cakes and sauna baths.

ASTRUC. And delightful young ladies too.

He winces at a percussive passage of piano.

But my dear Sergei Pavlovich, you are not going to allow this so-called ballet of Vaslav's to happen, are you?

DIAGHILEV. I am.

ASTRUC. Are you so *besotted* with him?

Pause. DIAGHILEV *turns on him slowly.*

DIAGHILEV (*in a cold rage*). If you are suggesting that I'm letting my emotions get the better of my artistic judgement, then our partnership is over.

ASTRUC. But why else are you doing this?

DIAGHILEV. Because what Vaslav is doing is revolutionary, and I believe in revolution. Most passionately I believe in it. And so does he. What other dancer in the world, who can soar like Icarus, would devise a form of dancing in which no dancer leaves the ground at all... in which they just... stamp?

The music from next door has stopped. NIJINSKY *comes in, casually dressed as for a workout, and pours himself a glass of water.*

ASTRUC. Stamping is not dancing.

DIAGHILEV. Explain to him, Vaslav.

NIJINSKY (*searching for words*). All movement is dancing, and dancing comes from God.

ASTRUC (*sighing*). Always God.

NIJINSKY. Yes. Always God. Even in primitive times there was God. *Le sacre de printemps* is a ballet of primitive man. He would dance – yes – but he would not greet the coming of spring with an *entrechat* or an arabesque. He would do none of that nonsense that they do at the Mariinsky.

He demonstrates a snatch of classic mime: hand on heart…

'I love…

Sideways scooping gesture:

… your beautiful face…

Finger on fourth finger of left hand:

… marry me!…

Hand ranges over a wide vista.

… all this will be yours.' No, no! His dance would be brutal, merciless, savage. He would greet the rebirth of the world by stamping!

NIJINSKY *stamps to make his point.*

ASTRUC. For an entire hour?

ASTRUC *indicates the door, through which the music has resumed.*

With Stravinsky's music the most discordant that even *he* has written? Sergei Pavlovich, we will have a disaster!

DIAGHILEV. A work of genius, dear Gabriel, may not get its instant reward, but it must be given its chance. After all, *L'après-midi d'un faune* was a success in the end...

ASTRUC.... only because of the scandal of Vaslav appearing to masturbate at the end.

(*To* NIJINSKY.) It will be bare feet again, I suppose?

NIJINSKY. Of course.

ASTRUC. But audiences *hate* bare feet!

NIJINSKY. And I hate audiences!

He's about to go back into the other room. DIAGHILEV *catches his hand.*

DIAGHILEV. May I not see what you are preparing?

NIJINSKY. Not till it's finished.

DIAGHILEV. Very well. Go and bring me the greatest masterpiece ever... *stamped.*

NIJINSKY *goes out.*

ASTRUC. Sometimes I think the boy is mad.

DIAGHILEV (*quietly*). Don't say that, please.

ASTRUC. Do you fear it too?

DIAGHILEV. His brother is mad... his grandmother too. But if Vaslav is mad, it's only in the sense that I am mad as well. We both have visions. Sometimes they are the same, sometimes different. But we share them, as we shared everything until recently.

ASTRUC. *C'est toi qui es fou.* And you are destroying your company with that other madness.

DIAGHILEV. Ah, yes... the matter of Fokine.

ASTRUC. It was insane of you to lose your principal choreographer.

DIAGHILEV. Fokine isn't *chic* any more. He's boring. Besides, he would have walked out anyway once Vaslav started making ballets of his own. Gabriel, I have given you three years of triumphs. Why draw back now from taking a little risk?

ASTRUC. But this ballet will cost a fortune.

DIAGHILEV. Our triumphs will pay for it.

ASTRUC. Our triumphs don't even pay for themselves. Last season we lost a million. This season will lose even more...

DIAGHILEV. Whatever we lose, we'll get back in London, with a handsome profit. You have my personal guarantee.

ASTRUC. Not that! Anything but your personal guarantee.

DIAGHILEV. Go with God, my Gabriel. Go!

He pushes ASTRUC *out of the door. Takes a look outside, closes the door and comes back in.*

Grigoriev.

GRIGORIEV. Sergei Pavlovich?

DIAGHILEV. There is a woman sitting in an armchair in the corridor. Would you ask her if she'd be good enough to come and see me?

GRIGORIEV. If she says no?

DIAGHILEV. She won't.

GRIGORIEV goes out. DIAGHILEV, *alone, glances at* GRIGORIEV's *figures before throwing them down angrily.* GRIGORIEV *comes back.*

GRIGORIEV (*announcing*). Mademoiselle Romola de Pulzky.

Another strain of Magyar music as ROMOLA DE PULZKY *comes in, a young woman with a calm mind and a strong will.* DIAGHILEV *nods to* GRIGORIEV *to go, and he does so.*

DIAGHILEV (*politely*). I know your face, Mademoiselle. I saw you drinking coffee in the Hotel Gellert yesterday morning, and last night you dined at the next table to us at the Tzigane. But I'm sorry to say that your name is not familiar.

ROMOLA. It should be, Monsieur Diaghilev. I've had the honour of entertaining nearly all your company here in Budapest. My mother is Emilia Markus, Hungary's most famous actress.

DIAGHILEV. I have heard of her, of course. Why are you following us, Mademoiselle?

ROMOLA. It's my ambition to be a dancer. I go to all your performances, all your rehearsals...

DIAGHILEV. How did you get into my *rehearsals*?

ROMOLA. I have a little money, a little influence... May I sit down?

DIAGHILEV. Of course, forgive me. But, Mademoiselle, flattered as I am by your enthusiasm for my ballet, that doesn't quite explain...

ROMOLA.... why I'm following you about? Well... as I worship the creation, should I not worship the creator? But from a distance, Monsieur Diaghilev. You need have no fear.

DIAGHILEV *laughs at this absurd attempt at flirtation.*

DIAGHILEV. Mademoiselle de Pulzky, you lie with great charm.

ROMOLA *inclines her head.*

No woman in her senses would follow me about. Which of my male dancers can it be? Is it... Nijinsky?

ROMOLA *laughs.*

ROMOLA. Nijinsky? As an artist he is incomparable. But what young woman would follow *him* about? I mean, what would be the purpose?

DIAGHILEV. Who do you favour, then?

ROMOLA. Apart from you?

DIAGHILEV (*dismissive*). My dear, that gambit is best forgotten. Tell me the truth.

ROMOLA. If you're determined to wring the secret of my heart from me... it's Adolph Bolm.

DIAGHILEV. Indeed?

ROMOLA. Adolph Bolm seems to me to be the personification of all that is most desirable in the male sex. Nijinsky may be a god, but he is without gender. Adolph Bolm is superbly masculine.

NIJINSKY comes suddenly into the room and goes up to DIAGHILEV, totally oblivious of ROMOLA.

NIJINSKY. Igor wants a bigger orchestra. Here's a list of the extra instruments we'll need.

ROMOLA is staring at him with admiration.

DIAGHILEV. Thank you, Vaslav. This is Mademoiselle Romola de Pulzky.

NIJINSKY (*doing his formal bow*). Mademoiselle.

DIAGHILEV. In her opinion, Adolph Bolm is the personification of manliness. While you, Vaslav... though a god... are without gender.

NIJINSKY looks at ROMOLA with interest.

NIJINSKY. But an artist should have no gender. Bolm is manly, true, but that is a fault. Art comes from God. Has God a gender? Is He male or female? Isn't He both?

ROMOLA has no answer, for a reason that will become clear later. NIJINSKY turns to DIAGHILEV.

Sergei Pavlovich, you will give Igor and me what we ask you for?

DIAGHILEV. You must both have whatever you want.

NIJINSKY smiles at him, gives another formal bow to ROMOLA and departs.

ROMOLA. It was cruel of you to quote me.

DIAGHILEV. I thought you didn't care for him.

ROMOLA. I care for him as an artist. The whole world does.

DIAGHILEV. But you have got rather closer to him than the whole world usually gets. Is it your plan to follow us to London?

ROMOLA. You can hardly stop me.

DIAGHILEV. On the contrary, I can encourage you. Such devotion from a lady with 'a little money and a little influence' is very heartening. Do you hope to join the company?

ROMOLA. Oh, I do. I've been wondering, for a start... Well, do you think Maestro Cecchetti would allow me to watch his classes?

DIAGHILEV. He will if I ask him to. He may even allow you to join in. Classes only with the *corps de ballet*, of course. The principals take their classes separately. And that includes your idol... Adolph Bolm.

ROMOLA (*shrugging*). I must accept my fate.

DIAGHILEV. All of us must. It's stronger than we are.

He puts out his hand.

Mademoiselle.

ROMOLA. I hope we'll meet again.

He opens the door for her.

DIAGHILEV. I'm sure we shall.

She goes. He dials a room number, and the call is answered.

Maestro Cecchetti? This is Sergei Pavlovich. I have invited a charming young amateur to attend your classes. But she is never, never to meet Vaslav alone. (*Pause.*) Not even accidental meetings on the stairs. You understand? It is imperative that you do as I say.

He rings off. Wonders: has he made a terrible mistake? He gets up thoughtfully, collects his hat, coat and stick, and goes.

'The Rite of Spring' is heard again from behind the doors, more thumpy and aggressively rhythmic than before. Now it

gets louder, sounding less like 'The Rite of Spring' than someone angrily banging the keys.

TERRY *appears from his bedroom, carrying a single shoe in one hand, but dressed; he's been asleep and is still only half-awake. He looks at the door, which is where the banging seems to be coming from.*

TERRY. What the fuck...?

The banging transforms itself into forceful knocking on the door. TERRY *looks at his watch. He's overslept.*

Shit.

(*Calls.*) Yes, I'm coming.

He opens the door to the sound of Magyar violins. OLD ROMOLA *is there. She's eighty but not at all frail. A forceful, determined old lady, not at all well-off, dowdily dressed, carrying an umbrella and a capacious bag.*

OLD ROMOLA. Sir Terence? I am Romola Nijinsky. I have been waiting for you in the lounge downstairs for the last half-hour.

TERRY. Well... I can join you there in a moment...

OLD ROMOLA. It is noisy in the lounge and I am hard of hearing. May we...?

She gestures past TERRY *towards his suite.*

TERRY. Yes, of course. Won't you come in?

He steps back and she comes into the room.

Do make yourself comfortable.

A chair.

I must apologise. It was most dreadfully rude of me to keep you waiting. I have a house in Bermuda, you see, and I only flew in to London this afternoon. Besides, I'm not on tip-top form at the moment. Nothing serious. All in hand. May I offer you a cup of tea?

He glances at his watch.

A glass of champagne?

OLD ROMOLA. Provided that it is of excellent quality, I would appreciate it.

TERRY *picks up the phone and dials.*

TERRY. Room service? Oh, Donald, yes, it's ah... Will you bring up a bottle of Dom Perignon and two glasses? Thank you.

(*To* OLD ROMOLA.) Is there anything else you need?

OLD ROMOLA. Only to rest my feet for a moment. I've had a tiresome afternoon. I walked and walked and the rain got heavier and it was quite impossible for me to find this hotel. Though I have been here before, during my husband's first London season. With him, of course, and Lady Ottoline Morrell and Mr Bertrand Russell. But now the roads in London have all been changed. I had to hail a taxi and his fee was quite absurd. But we must talk about your play.

TERRY. Oh, absolutely.

He shifts uneasily, as she gets out a battered copy of the script plus letters, notebooks and coloured pencils, and arranges them before her.

OLD ROMOLA. I hope you did not regard my letters to you as too intemperate. If you create a play out of your own imagination, then what you write is up to you. But if you choose to depict characters who existed in life... and, what is more, who existed in living memory... then it is your duty to be accurate. And whether the imagination of one man can create an accurate picture of a genius, I somewhat doubt. I am sure you understand.

TERRY, *unprepared for this approach, is briefly lost for words. Then:*

TERRY. I'll get my script.

He goes to his bedroom door and opens it to reveal a wild and noisy Russian party going on inside. People are singing, a balalaika is playing, glasses are being smashed, and people are dancing to a stamping rhythm. TERRY *glances back at* OLD ROMOLA, *but she pays no attention; the party is not in her world. She is preoccupied with consulting her notes.*

TERRY *goes into the bedroom to a chorus of drunken welcomes, disregarding all invitations to join in, and emerges with his screenplay and carrying both his shoes.*

You were saying?

OLD ROMOLA. It may save some time if I inform you that I have written a detailed memorandum to Mr Carter and Mr Ruck...

TERRY. Carter-Ruck. One person. Yes, he sent me a copy. If I read it correctly, your main complaint is that I've...

OLD ROMOLA. It is not a *complaint.* It is the *correction* of an *error.*

TERRY. What's the error?

OLD ROMOLA. It's your depiction of myself as a calculating little minx who plots to entrap Nijinsky in marriage.

TERRY. Oh, now where would that be, I wonder?

OLD ROMOLA. Page twenty-five.

TERRY. You and Diaghilev?

OLD ROMOLA. Exactly.

TERRY *finds and looks at it.*

TERRY. This scene was a joy to write. I was playing Puccini in the background and it practically wrote itself. And I really don't see it the way that you do. I don't think anyone would. A young woman of nineteen sees a dancer of genius... she worships him from afar... and she plans an amusing little stratagem in order to get to know him.

A knock at the door and DONALD *comes in with champagne and glasses.*

Oh, thank you.

He continues, as DONALD *opens the bottle and pours, placing one foot carefully on* TERRY*'s foot... the one, that is, that hasn't yet got a shoe on it.*

May I be honest with you? I've never written a truly great play. I wish I had. I long to write a *Hamlet* or a *Hedda Gabler* before I... before I die. But if I don't, I'll still have nothing to be ashamed of. I've never lied in a play. I've never 'faked it'. I write the truth, as it seems to me. And fortunately for me, it's been recognised as the truth by many... many thousands of theatregoers...

The pressure of DONALD*'s foot is putting him off his stroke, but continues nevertheless.*

... rich and poor and, and, and middle class, which I know is a horrifically unfashionable thing to be these days...

He decisively moves his foot away.

... and I write about women with what some people have kindly said is remarkable insight. I think I know how you felt when you fell in love. You knew that in order to get what you wanted, you would have to fight for it. Why shouldn't you fight? What's wrong with that? I hope that satisfies you.

DONALD (*about to go*). Will that be all for now, sir?

TERRY. That will be all.

DONALD *goes.*

(*To* OLD ROMOLA.) Of course, if there's any adjustment that you'd like me to make, I'll be happy to hear it.

OLD ROMOLA (*ferociously*). It is not an adjustment! It's the whole of the scene! It is suggested here that I am making a vulgar attempt to start a love affair with Nijinsky. And it *never entered my head* that I might do so.

TERRY. So you didn't trick Diaghilev into inviting you to attend Cecchetti's class?

OLD ROMOLA. No, I did not!

TERRY. What if I say you did?

OLD ROMOLA. Then I shall sue you!

TERRY. *Sue* me?

OLD ROMOLA. Yes!

TERRY. For saying you wanted to marry the man you loved?

OLD ROMOLA. For saying I plotted to do so like a prostitute!

TERRY. Well, if it should come to legal action, I've got something here that I think any judge would be very interested to read.

OLD ROMOLA. You show me!

TERRY. I will. I certainly will.

He produces a book.

(Reads the cover.) Nijinsky by Romola Nijinsky.

He finds the page, already bookmarked.

(Reads.) 'Diaghilev smiled amiably, and he agreed that I could go to class with the celebrated Maestro Cecchetti. I left his hotel room in a haze of excitement. My plot had succeeded! I could hardly believe that I had fooled...' *fooled...* 'such a clever and crafty man as Sergei Diaghilev.'

He sits back in satisfaction.

You did write this?

No reply.

Well, there we are. May I suggest that we enjoy our champagne and bask in happy memories? And please, let's have no more nonsense about my screenplay.

He drinks. OLD ROMOLA *is thoughtful.*

Are you still living in Paris?

She nods.

I try to get over once or twice a year. Of course, it's never been the same since the war.

She's still thoughtful.

I do hope that you'll be able to see some of the filming. You could write a little piece about it for *The Times*. I'm sure they'd print it. I could recommend it to the editor, if you liked.

OLD ROMOLA. There is one more thing that I cannot allow.

TERRY (*with irony*). Allow?

OLD ROMOLA. You suggest that Nijinsky and Diaghilev had a homosexual affair.

TERRY. And?

OLD ROMOLA. That is a slander.

TERRY. You're not serious?

OLD ROMOLA. I am entirely serious.

TERRY. Are you suggesting that they *didn't* have…?

OLD ROMOLA. Of course they didn't!

TERRY. But Nijinsky says in his diaries…

OLD ROMOLA. … when he was mentally disturbed!

TERRY. They shared train compartments. They shared hotel rooms. They shared *beds*.

OLD ROMOLA. It was cheaper that way.

TERRY. This is ridiculous. There are witnesses who'll swear that…

OLD ROMOLA. My husband's love for Diaghilev was not a *physical* love. It was an *artistic* love, a *spiritual* love. It was the love of an artist for the man who provides his inspiration.

I was *married* to Nijinsky. I *know* the truth. If you suggest otherwise, I shall take legal action.

TERRY. On what grounds?

OLD ROMOLA. Criminal libel.

TERRY. Madame Nijinsky, I hate to disappoint you, but homosexual acts have been perfectly legal in this country since 1967.

OLD ROMOLA. They were not legal *then*!

TERRY. That isn't the point. You cannot libel the dead. It's a fundamental principle of English law. You haven't the *vestige* of a case. If you try to sue, you won't get a penny and you'll be saddled with the costs.

OLD ROMOLA. It will not be my money! There are people who have a reverence for my husband. *Wealthy* people. *Titled* people. It is *they* who will pay the legal bills, and *I* who will have the pleasure of facing you in court, when I proclaim to the judge and jury and the newspapers and the radio and the television... what kind of person you are.

TERRY. Which is what?

OLD ROMOLA. Why would you throw mud at my husband, if not to make your own mud seem cleaner?

TERRY. I beg your pardon?

OLD ROMOLA. I've read your interviews in the newspapers. 'Oh, Sir Terence, why have you never married?' 'Well, it's hard to say,' you answer. 'Maybe the right woman never came along.'

She laughs heartily and helps herself to a peanut.

The right woman! What kind of woman would she be, I wonder? You are a *pervert*! It is obvious in your face, your eyes, your smile, your walk...

She bangs her copy of the screenplay on the table with some force.

... and in every degenerate word you write. If this play is produced, I will expose you to all the world as a man of bestial proclivities. Is that quite clear?

She gets up and collects her things.

Thank you for the champagne.

She downs it in a gulp.

I have had better.

She goes. TERRY, *deeply shaken, watches her go.*

TERRY. Jesus Christ.

DIAGHILEV. I told you she was a monster.

DIAGHILEV *goes to a connecting door and knocks. No answer. He goes to the telephone. Dials a room number.*

Grigoriev? You have a key to Monsieur Nijinsky's bedroom, do you not? Good. Go to his room now, open the door from the corridor and say I sent you. If he is ill, which I fear, bring me news.

He rings off. Turns to TERRY.

The catastrophe is drawing closer.

TERRY. It certainly is.

We hear a key turn and NIJINSKY *comes in via the connecting door. He is in pyjamas and dressing gown and stands before* DIAGHILEV, *looking rather like a penitent schoolboy.*

DIAGHILEV. Were you asleep?

NIJINSKY. You know I don't sleep.

DIAGHILEV. Sometimes you do. And you might have been tired, after your work with Stravinsky.

NIJINSKY. Oh yes, I am tired. But it's not just that...

DIAGHILEV (*gently*). Are you ill again, Vatzka?

NIJINSKY. I had a terrible vision.

DIAGHILEV. What was it?

NIJINSKY. You were dead and I was still alive.

DIAGHILEV. Well... by the odds, that is likely.

NIJINSKY. But I wasn't really alive. I was alive, but somehow I was dead too... but so much worse than dead.

He shivers.

DIAGHILEV. Do you see it happening soon?

NIJINSKY. Very soon.

DIAGHILEV. In London?

NIJINSKY *shakes his head slowly.*

Perhaps after London? In South America?

NIJINSKY. Maybe between London and South America.

DIAGHILEV. Between the two is the Atlantic Ocean... and I won't be travelling on the ship. I'm putting the Baron de Gunzburg in charge of the company.

NIJINSKY. You're frightened of the sea, aren't you?

DIAGHILEV. I am. A fortune-teller in Russia told me that my life would end on water.

Superstitiously, he crosses himself.

Besides, I must stay and work on our next season.

NIJINSKY. Come on the boat. Then if you drown, I'll drown with you. It would be best for our lives to end together.

DIAGHILEV. Don't be morbid.

NIJINSKY *looks at the champagne.*

NIJINSKY. Can I have a glass of champagne?

DIAGHILEV. It isn't good for you.

NIJINSKY. It's to give me courage.

DIAGHILEV. You need courage... with me?

NIJINSKY. Tonight, I do.

DIAGHILEV. Then so do I.

He pours two glasses and they drink. NIJINSKY *crouches on a stool, like a deer on a rock. After a moment:*

NIJINSKY. There are things that I have to say to you. But I'm bad with words. I have feelings, great feelings… but I can't express them. I have emotion without understanding and that is a bad thing.

He puts his hand on DIAGHILEV's *knee, which is close by.* DIAGHILEV *lets it rest there before gently moving it.*

DIAGHILEV. Try to tell me.

NIJINSKY. For the last four years I have been a part of you, and happy and proud to be that. I have been your creation and a creation is at one with his creator. You have given me life, and I bless you for it, revere you for it… love you for it. For ever and ever, Sergei Pavlovich, for ever and ever, Amen.

Emotion getting the better of him, he holds out his glass. DIAGHILEV *takes it and refills it.* NIJINSKY *furtively wipes his eyes.*

But now that I am a creator myself…

DIAGHILEV (*harshly*). Who made you into a creator?

NIJINSKY. You did. It was the best, the kindest, the noblest act you ever did. Don't think I don't know what it cost you to lose Fokine.

DIAGHILEV (*still harshly*). Don't cry, or I'll cry… and we'll have that familiar spectacle, so funny to the rest of the world, of two Slavs sobbing on each other's shoulders for no reason at all. Drink this.

NIJINSKY *takes it and gulps it, recovering after a moment.*

NIJINSKY. This is what I must say to you. Now that I am a creator myself, I don't any longer need you in the way that I did. I must belong to myself and no one else. Not even you.

DIAGHILEV (*intensely*). No one else? You mean that?

NIJINSKY. There could never be anyone else. I swear it on my mother's head.

DIAGHILEV. Your mother is a sick woman. Let me have it on your own head.

NIJINSKY. On my own head.

DIAGHILEV *smiles, takes* NIJINSKY's *hand, pulls him to his feet and propels him gently towards the connecting door.*

DIAGHILEV. Go to bed. You need rest.

NIJINSKY. You are a great and good man and I love you. And only you.

DIAGHILEV. For ever and ever.

NIJINSKY (*smiling*). Amen.

DIAGHILEV (*with gentle reproof*). But, Vatzka... no more locked doors.

NIJINSKY *swings the door open, takes the key out of the lock and gives it to him.* DIAGHILEV *kisses him paternally on the head.*

Goodnight.

NIJINSKY. Goodnight.

DIAGHILEV. And don't be frightened about the ballet.

NIJINSKY. I'm very frightened.

DIAGHILEV. It will be a triumph. On that you have my personal guarantee.

NIJINSKY *smiles and goes.* DIAGHILEV *waits a moment, then quietly, firmly turns the key in the lock.* TERRY *is lying back, looking miserable.*

(*To* TERRY.) Shall we go on?

TERRY (*distracted*). What? Oh yes. Thursday May 29th 1913.

ATTENDANTS *take their places in the foyer.*

As before, I suggest we *hear* the event as opposed to seeing
it…

DIAGHILEV. No, no, no!

He hustles the ATTENDANTS *out.*

I don't want to hear a single whistle, a single boo, a single
catcall from the gallery. Do not believe one word you have
heard about that evening! If everyone who claims to have
seen *The Rite of Spring* was really there, it would have been
danced to a million people.

A chorus of boos is heard. DIAGHILEV *puts his hands over
his ears.*

Stop, stop, stop!

It stops abruptly, like an artificial effect. ASTRUC
approaches angrily.

ASTRUC. Well, you can't say I didn't warn you…

DIAGHILEV. But I *can* say, 'Get off this stage and stop
depressing my dancers!'

ASTRUC *stomps off, then comes back. Meanwhile:*

(*To* TERRY.) It may be that the whistling began in the first
five bars of music. It may be that the audience fought duels
with their umbrellas. It may be that the police were called. It
may be that Vaslav stood on a chair in the wings, screaming
'one, two, three' to the dancers who were unable to hear a
word above the noise. *That* I remember. It's also true that
when somebody asked me how I felt, I answered, 'It is
exactly what I wanted.' Which was the greatest lie of my life.

ASTRUC *comes back.*

ASTRUC. You realise that this will bankrupt me?

DIAGHILEV. Gabriel, Gabriel, what is a little bankruptcy,
measured against your name in history as the man who
helped to create a masterpiece…?

ASTRUC *stomps off again.*

Then I saw Nijinsky.

He sees NIJINSKY *standing apart, his face a mask.*

Vaslav.

NIJINSKY. Yes?

DIAGHILEV. You are a choreographer of genius.

NIJINSKY. I know.

DIAGHILEV. But it will be another century before such choreography is accepted.

NIJINSKY. But it *will* be accepted.

DIAGHILEV. Oh, it will.

NIJINSKY. And *Joseph* will be even better.

DIAGHILEV. '*Joseph*'?

NIJINSKY. My next dance. *The Legend of Joseph.* To the music by Richard Strauss. I've been working on it for months. I've told you about it every day.

DIAGHILEV. Of course you have. A wonderful subject. We must talk about it further. Now… go to dinner with the others. I'll join you soon.

　　NIJINSKY *kisses him chastely, and goes.* GRIGORIEV *is in the background.*

Grigoriev?

GRIGORIEV *comes forward.*

GRIGORIEV. Sergei Pavlovich?

DIAGHILEV *glances at* TERRY.

TERRY. Say it.

DIAGHILEV (*to* GRIGORIEV). Somebody told me that Fokine was in the audience.

GRIGORIEV. He was. I saw him.

DIAGHILEV. Go quickly. Find him. Tell him I wish to speak with him. He will know what it's about.

GRIGORIEV *goes*. DIAGHILEV *stays*.

End of Act One.

ACT TWO

As before, TERRY*'s suite at Claridge's.* TERRY *and his mother,*
VERA RATTIGAN, *are having tea.* VERA, *once a beauty, now
in her seventies, is dressed for coming up to London and has
shopping bags beside her.*

VERA (*shocked*). But, darling, what are you saying? Has the
BBC turned down your play?

TERRY. No, Mother, of course they haven't. They'd never do
that. It's just that…

VERA. What?

TERRY. Well, it's rather upsetting. You see, there's somebody
who doesn't like the play and it's just possible that she'll
create some awful difficulty. I've not even sure that I want it
to be made. I might withdraw it.

VERA. And I was *so* looking forward to it. I saw Nijinsky
dance, as I'm sure I've told you.

TERRY. No, you've never told me that.

VERA. Well, darling, I hardly see you. You were two. I
remember the date quite clearly, because your father was
back on leave. He and I had an early supper at the Café
Royal and then we went to Covent Garden to see the Russian
Ballet.

TERRY. What did he dance?

VERA. Well, I seem to remember a ballet with some rather
inconclusive music in which they all did peculiar things with
their hands.

*She mimes, face and hands in profile, like Egyptian
hieroglyphics.*

TERRY. *L'après-midi d'un faune*.

VERA. I expect it was. Your father told me afterwards that Nijinsky did something rather unnecessary towards the end, but I wasn't looking at that point. And then *Petrouchka*, which I didn't enjoy. He had a hideous halfwit make-up on his face and he didn't do those wonderful leaps that one used to read about. He... Well, I don't know what to call it exactly. He lolloped.

TERRY. Lolloped?

VERA. Like a puppet.

TERRY. Petrouchka *is* a puppet.

VERA. I'm not saying it wasn't *truthful*, but why does the truth have to be so *ugly*? Is it so wrong of one to want a little more *beauty* in one's life? I know you'll think I'm a hopeless lowbrow.

TERRY. Mother darling, if it weren't for people like you, I'd be selling vacuum cleaners door to door. And since you and I are getting on so well, why don't you come to Maggie Leighton's first night with me next week?

VERA. Well, if you're quite certain it won't be boring for you.

TERRY *winces, then takes a swig of his painkiller.*

What's that?

TERRY. It's nothing, darling. Don't let your tea get cold.

VERA *sips her tea.*

VERA. We saw the Russian Ballet again the following year, but Nijinsky wasn't in it.

TERRY. No, he'd been sacked.

VERA. Why was that?

TERRY. He'd got married, and Diaghilev didn't approve.

VERA. He sacked him because of that?

TERRY. More or less.

VERA. Russians are so emotional, aren't they? You'd think Diaghilev would be *pleased* that his friend was happily settled down. Though on the other hand, one does hear rumours about the world of ballet.

TERRY *stirs his tea, or does whatever he can to avoid being drawn further.*

That reminds me. I've been meaning to ask you something...

TERRY. Oh yes?

VERA.... but you're not to accuse me of intruding in your private life.

TERRY (*edgily*). Mm-hm?

VERA. I'm not a bigoted woman. I may be old, but I try to keep up with the times.

TERRY. Oh, you do.

VERA. And as your mother, I feel that I ought to accept however you choose to lead your life, and not to be silly and shocked about it.

TERRY. Mother, what *is* it?

VERA. Are you...? No, I mustn't interfere.

TERRY. Go on!

VERA. Are you in love with Maggie? And if you are, don't you think the two of you should be getting married?

TERRY *stares at her in surprise, then giggles.*

TERRY. Mother... Maggie is just a friend.

VERA *sighs sadly.*

VERA. That is *exactly* what your father would have said.

TERRY. Well...

Whatever he was going to say is drowned by the loud hoot of a ship about to pull away from the quayside. Maybe a gangplank is wheeled on. Noise of seagulls. PORTERS *with*

luggage and PASSENGERS *swarm past, having just
embarked on board. An arrow indicates 'Second Class'.*
TERRY *observes all this with resigned bewilderment.*

… darling, I'm quite worn out. Would you mind awfully if
I…

VERA. Of course, you've had a long journey. When I see you
again, you must tell me all about Bermuda. I suppose
everything there happens very late.

TERRY. What, late at night?

VERA. No, I mean that if you order a cup of tea, it doesn't
arrive for half an hour because they're all living it up in the
kitchen. You needn't show me to the lift, my darling. Give
me a kiss.

By now, TERRY *has shown her to the door, she being
unconscious of the activity buzzing around her. They kiss and
she goes.* TERRY *takes a seat on a deckchair, in the same
world as all those on the voyage.*

ROMOLA *appears with her maid,* ANNA, *walking
purposefully in the opposite direction to the 'Second Class'
arrow. The* SHIP'S PURSER *appears.*

ROMOLA. Purser! Purser! Can I have your attention, please!

PURSER. Yes, Miss de Pulzky? What can I do for you?

ROMOLA. How many days will it be before we get to Buenos
Aires?

PURSER. It is a twenty-one-day voyage, Mademoiselle de
Pulzky.

ROMOLA. Twenty-one days in second class! That's quite
impossible for me. I must change my cabin. Besides, you
know, I have a great personal friend travelling first class, and
I want to be as near as possible to him.

PURSER. And what is the name of this great personal friend?

ROMOLA. Monsieur Nijinsky.

PURSER (*surprised*). Monsieur Nijinsky? He is travelling in…

He checks.

…B60 and 61, in a combined suite with the Baron de Gunzburg. I can give you B65. It's an inside cabin, but it is opposite. It will cost you another forty-eight pounds.

ROMOLA. I'll take it.

She opens her bag and gets out banknotes. BALLET GIRLS *and* BOYS *appear, trouping towards the 'Second Class' arrow.* ADOLPH BOLM, *tall, handsome and manly, comes up to* ROMOLA *with a broad smile and kisses her.*

BOLM. My dear little Romola, how wonderful that you are sailing with us.

ROMOLA (*coolly*). Good morning, Monsieur Bolm. I'm afraid that I won't be seeing you on the voyage. I am travelling first class.

BOLM. Who can jump the barrier between second and first more easily than me? I hope to see you every day… (*Meaningfully.*) and every night.

ROMOLA. Well, we must see how things go, mustn't we?

(*To the* PURSER, *having passed over the money.*) Fifty pounds. Keep the change.

(*To* BOLM.) Forgive me, Adolph, but I can't stay talking with you. I have an invitation to cocktails.

BOLM. Cocktails?

ROMOLA. It is the trend, you know. These days one must always be in the trend!

A PORTER *appears and she indicates her cabin luggage, which he carries out in the opposite direction to the 'Second Class' arrow. Two* BALLET GIRLS *pass and call to* BOLM:

BALLET GIRLS. Adolph! Adolph! Come with us. We're having a party in cabin 6!

BOLM *follows them with a will;* ROMOLA *was no big deal after all. She is about to go, but the appearance of* NIJINSKY *and* BARON DE GUNZBURG, *with* PORTERS *and luggage, slows down her exit.* GUNZBURG *is a decadent dandy with aesthetic pretensions.* ROMOLA *steps forward as* ANNA *tactfully leaves.*

ROMOLA. Good morning, Baron de Gunzburg. Good morning, Monsieur Nijinsky.

NIJINSKY / GUNZBERG. Good morning.

ROMOLA. I believe you are taking Sergei Pavlovich's place on this voyage, Baron?

GUNZBURG. He has put me in charge of the tour. But I'm afraid that I don't...

He looks at her more closely.

... ah, now I remember. Aren't you the young lady who's been attending Maestro Cecchetti's classes?

ROMOLA. I am! I hope I'll soon have a place in the corps de ballet. Monsieur Nijinsky...

NIJINSKY *turns to her for the first time.*

I... have been given the cabin opposite to yours. We'll be seeing a lot of each other on this trip.

No reply.

Well... I must find my cabin, I suppose. Goodbye!

She goes, flustered.

GUNZBURG. What is her name?

NIJINSKY. I've no idea.

GUNZBURG. She's very pretty.

NIJINSKY. Do you think so?

GUNZBURG. Don't you? You needn't answer. I know you will always be loyal to Sergei Pavlovich.

NIJINSKY (*frowning*). You're one of his closest friends, aren't you?

GUNZBURG *nods, smiling. Lights a cigar.*

I know you're his principal Russian backer.

GUNZBURG. I think I can claim to have lost more money on his behalf than any of his French Rothschilds. Although I do not regret the loss of a single franc. I thought your Stravinsky ballet was a magnificent work.

NIJINSKY (*stiffly*). Thank you.

GUNZBURG. Has Sergei Pavlovich asked you to follow it up with another?

NIJINSKY. Not yet.

GUNZBURG. How strange. That is what *I* would ask you to do, if your contract was with me, and not with him.

NIJINSKY. I don't have a contract.

GUNZBURG. Only a verbal contract?

NIJINSKY. Not even that.

GUNZBURG. But that's a scandal! Your agent ought to insist...

NIJINSKY. I don't have an agent.

GUNZBURG. Then who negotiates your fees?

NIJINSKY. I don't get fees. In three years, I have never received a rouble from Sergei Pavlovich.

GUNZBURG. But that's disgraceful! Just consider how much he owes you...

NIJINSKY. What he owes me is much less than I owe him.

GUNZBURG. Then you obviously don't know your own worth. May I put my cards on the table? I am planning to start a ballet company of my own. I would consider it the greatest honour if you would consider...

NIJINSKY. Baron, I would never join your company.

GUNZBURG. No?

NIJINSKY. No, never. I will never work for anyone except for Sergei Pavlovich.

The STEWARD *appears.*

STEWARD. May I show you to your suite, gentlemen?

GUNZBURG (*to* NIJINSKY). After you.

They go. TERRY *reads to himself from his script. Meanwhile,* ROMOLA *appears and throws herself down into a deckchair.* ANNA *follows, bringing* ROMOLA*'s bag.*

TERRY. 'As the days go by, we see, in a series of swift flashes, Romola walking repeatedly past Nijinsky's deckchair, lingering as she does so to flash him...

He rewrites a word.

... *throw* him a glance or smile, but she receives no further acknowledgement, da da da...'

He puts in another tiny rewrite. ANNA *is filing and polishing her nails.*

ANNA. Does Mademoiselle require anything else?

ROMOLA (*irritably*). You know exactly what Mademoiselle requires. Oh, it's too awful, Anna! He completely ignores me!

ANNA. Well, you know our old Hungarian saying? 'There's no sense in running after a hay cart that won't give you a lift.'

ROMOLA. But it's only a little shipboard flirtation! That isn't too much to ask, is it?

ANNA. It's too much to ask of him.

ROMOLA. You're right. Diaghilev has him, body and soul. Body and soul... it's too depressing. Anna, why don't you go back to second class for the rest of the morning. You can come back after lunch.

ANNA. Thank you, Mademoiselle.

She goes. Seagulls are heard. ROMOLA *looks round, bored. She glances at* TERRY. *Gives him a polite smile, then sees* DONALD *approaching with a drink on a tray.*

ROMOLA. Oh, I've been waiting for this for hours!

DONALD. I'm sorry, Madame. It's very busy down in the lounge.

She takes the Martini.

Oh, and Sir Terence... There's a Mr Messina from the BBC waiting for you downstairs.

TERRY. Tell him to come up.

DONALD. Certainly, sir.

DONALD *goes.* TERRY *pages a little further through his script.*

TERRY. This will be tricky.

GUNZBURG *appears behind* ROMOLA.

GUNZBURG. May I join you?

ROMOLA*'s eyes widen. Her heart is fluttering. Can this be* NIJINSKY *at last?*

ROMOLA. Who's that?

GUNZBURG. Baron de Gunzburg.

She turns and sees him.

ROMOLA. Oh, it's you. Yes, if you want.

She pats the deckchair beside her. He sits and proceeds.

GUNZBURG. Mademoiselle...

ROMOLA. Yes?

GUNZBURG.... forgive me if I seem to be insulting. I don't mean to be, but if you find me so, you must tell me to go and I will.

ROMOLA (*cautiously*). Go on?

GUNZBURG. Walking backwards and forwards past his deckchair is no good at all.

ROMOLA. You've *noticed*?

GUNZBURG. It's rather hard not to.

ROMOLA. Has *he*?

GUNZBURG. Of course.

ROMOLA. Oh God! Does it annoy him?

GUNZBURG. Not at all. He thinks you're a very beautiful girl…

ROMOLA (*eagerly*). He said that?

GUNZBURG. Many times. And a very attractive girl.

ROMOLA. Then why doesn't he…?

GUNZBURG. You must use psychology, Mademoiselle. Vaslav Nijinsky has been pursued, since he was seventeen, by countless people of both sexes.

ROMOLA. And he responds only to one of them and it isn't mine. Is that what you're saying?

GUNZBURG. Not at all. He's still a shy and simple-minded boy. He responds to no one.

ROMOLA. Not even Diaghilev?

GUNZBURG. Diaghilev is his creator. Don't we all make some response to our creator, even if it is only an act of homage? I propose that you try more *direct* tactics.

ROMOLA (*explosively*). But I have! And I've *always* failed. I've been introduced to him countless times and he looks right through me! He doesn't even know my name.

GUNZBURG. He does now.

ROMOLA. Because you've told him?

GUNZBURG. Yes.

ROMOLA. He'll have forgotten it by tomorrow.

GUNZBURG. I think not.

ROMOLA. Why?

GUNZBERG stands straight and practically clicks his heels.

GUNZBURG. Mademoiselle de Pulzky, will you do me the honour of being my guest tomorrow night at the Fancy Dress Ball?

ROMOLA. Will *he* be there?

GUNZBURG. He will be your partner.

ROMOLA. Oh God! And I wasn't even planning to go. What should I wear?

GUNZBURG. Might I make a little suggestion?

He whispers it in her ear. She looks shocked.

ROMOLA. But...

GUNZBURG. It will calm his fears.

ROMOLA. But how will I talk to him? I only speak Hungarian and French. What does he speak?

GUNZBURG. Only Russian and Polish. But believe me, young lady, there are situations where words are no longer needed. Until tonight.

He goes. CEDRIC MESSINA appears on deck. He's a big, loud man; handsome, lived-in face, catty manner. He's played by the same actor who plays DIAGHILEV. ROMOLA stays on deck, doing her nails.

CEDRIC. Hello, Terry! Welcome back.

TERRY. Hello, Cedric. I'm sorry to drag you all the way up here. I was having a skim through the play.

CEDRIC. How did it seem?

TERRY. I think it's even better than I remembered.

He reaches for his bottle of whisky.

Can I pour you a drink?

CEDRIC. Yes, why not.

He downs the glass he brought up from the bar, gives
TERRY *his glass to refill and sits.*

How was the flight?

TERRY. It was perfectly fine until they started showing the film.
Guess what it was? *Bequest to the Nation.* My God, what a
stinker.

CEDRIC. Why do you write for those appalling people?

TERRY. Why do you think? It's my ridiculous lifestyle. I've got
a house in Bermuda, a house in Brighton and a mansion in
Scotland that I don't imagine I'll ever spend a single night in.

CEDRIC. One never knows.

TERRY. Actually, I think sometimes one does know.

Pause. Seagulls squawk overhead.

CEDRIC. Am I meant to understand something by that remark?

TERRY. Oh, I see what you mean!

He laughs.

No, no, no! I mean, come on, Cedric, given the life I've led,
the fags and the booze and all the rest of it, do you think I'd
be sitting here today, if I weren't a survivor? I'm tough as
old boots. I'm good for years. So for God's sake, don't let
your American producer friends get the impression that I'm
on my way out, or they'll be crossing me off their lists and I
need the work.

CEDRIC. You see, I'd heard that…

TERRY. Let's drop it, shall we? I've just seen Romola.

CEDRIC. What's she like?

TERRY. Well, not at all like I expected. She's not a *grande
dame* for a start. She wore a peculiar motley collection of old
clothes. I think she's probably on her uppers. But very astute.
And stubborn as hell. She hates the script.

CEDRIC. We all know that.

TERRY. Yes, but it's *what* she hates that's so surprising.

CEDRIC. Which is?

TERRY. Well, it's Nijinsky and Diaghilev having an affair.

CEDRIC *stares at him in surprise.*

CEDRIC. They did.

TERRY. She says they didn't.

CEDRIC *laughs raucously.*

Yes, well, obviously she's deluded, but she's convinced herself so I suppose it's just possible that she could convince other people as well.

CEDRIC. Like who?

TERRY. The press?

CEDRIC. *They* won't care.

TERRY. What about a jury?

CEDRIC. A jury? Terry, what is all this? If the stupid old bat takes us to court, she won't have a leg to stand on.

TERRY. Yes, I know, but...

CEDRIC. Not a *femur.*

TERRY. Cedric, listen. Don't you think that a case like that would reflect rather badly on the good name of the BBC?

CEDRIC. We haven't got a good name. The public hates us. They think we're a bunch of poofs and pinkos. Why don't you stop inventing problems and listen to what I have to say to you?

TERRY. Yes, all right.

CEDRIC *takes the script and uses it for emphasis.*

CEDRIC. You've written a wonderful screenplay here. It has suspense, it has a ripping good story and it has profound and

truthful things to say about the nature of love. Everyone at
the Beeb's gone wild about it. And the upshot is, we want it
to go into production in three months' time.

TERRY. Isn't that very soon?

CEDRIC. It is, and I'll tell you why, but you must keep it under
your chic *chapeau*.

TERRY. Mm-hm?

CEDRIC. I've got something very big coming up at the Beeb.

TERRY. Oh yes?

CEDRIC. A three-year project.

TERRY. Gosh.

CEDRIC. So what do you think it is?

TERRY. I can't imagine.

CEDRIC. Well, it's an international first, old chum. They want
me to produce every one of Shakespeare's plays on television.

TERRY. In a single series?

CEDRIC. Yes!

TERRY. Well, that *is* big.

CEDRIC. It's more than big. It's bloody immense. There are
thirty-seven of the fuckers. I don't want to blow my trumpet,
Terry, but this is something I'll be remembered for, for a
very long time. That's why I want to slot in your little epic
first, before the other thing gets going.

TERRY. Have you considered who might direct it?

CEDRIC. I'll do it myself. I assume you're happy with that.

TERRY. Oh yes.

CEDRIC. I've got some very exciting ideas about the casting.

TERRY. Oh yes?

CEDRIC. Diaghilev… Alan Badel, Scofield or Alan Bates.

TERRY. Fine.

CEDRIC. Peter Firth or Michael Kitchen as Nijinsky. Romola I don't know... Felicity Kendal?

Pause.

Terry, what's the problem?

TERRY. Well, the problem is *old* Romola. She really doesn't want this to happen.

CEDRIC. I thought you were going to tell her to take a flying fuck at a rolling doughnut.

TERRY. It's not as easy as that.

CEDRIC. I'll tell her *for* you if you like.

TERRY. No, don't do that. You see... she says that, if we film this script, she isn't only going to sue the BBC. She's going to take it out on me in the most atrocious way.

CEDRIC. Which is what?

TERRY. She's going to publicly denounce me.

CEDRIC. What as?

TERRY. You know what as.

CEDRIC. No, I don't.

TERRY. As... 'that'.

CEDRIC. As *what*?

TERRY. As what the entire play's about!

CEDRIC. A ballet dancer?

TERRY. No, a *queer*!

CEDRIC *looks bemused.*

She's going to tell the world that I'm a pervert with bestial proclivities.

CEDRIC. This is the problem?

TERRY. Yes!

There are tears of anger and frustration in his eyes.

God, I hate this. It's all such shit. One gets it all one's life, one way or another. Thank your lucky stars you're a heterosexual.

He gets out a handkerchief and blows his nose. Somewhere about here, ROMOLA *goes out towards her cabin.* CEDRIC *thoughtfully pours himself another whisky.*

CEDRIC (*kindly*). Terry…

TERRY (*bitterly*). What?

CEDRIC. Just leaving aside the bestial whatsits… which are none of my business…

TERRY. I haven't got any, all right?

CEDRIC. I'm not saying you do…

TERRY. Well, don't!

CEDRIC. Calm down. If we just concentrate for a moment on the queer thing… which is what I assume it all boils down to…

TERRY. Well?

CEDRIC (*still kindly*)…. you're sixty-three years old. You've never married. You've been photographed in a succession of elegant drawing rooms, wearing either a well-cut suit or a silk dressing gown, with your Sobranie cigarette delicately poised in an amber holder…

TERRY. Look, I know what you're saying!

CEDRIC…. can there be anyone in Britain who doesn't already know? Apart from some nice old lady with a parrot in Cheltenham?

TERRY. That isn't the point.

CEDRIC. Why not?

TERRY. Because it *isn't*. It simply isn't. You've just got to take my word for it.

CEDRIC. Are you worried about your mother?

Of two PASSENGERS *strolling past, one turns and is revealed to be* VERA.

VERA (*to* TERRY). I've been dead and buried for the last three years. He ought to *know* that!

TERRY (*very upset by this*). My mother's dead.

CEDRIC. Then I can't for the life of me see what you're panicking about!

TERRY. I won't be *categorised*. I refuse to be *this* kind of person or *that* kind of person. It would diminish me.

CEDRIC. That's all bollocks.

TERRY. Well, it's how it is, and I can't do anything about it.

CEDRIC *suddenly grasps what* TERRY *doesn't dare to say.*

CEDRIC. You're not saying that you want me to pull the play?

Pause.

Are you?

Pause.

Oh, Jesus Christ.

TERRY. Look, I've had a rough time. You *know* that. It's been thirteen years since anything of mine really took off. *Thirteen fucking years.* With Tynan being a complete and utter shit in the *Observer*. And the rest of them not much better. While pompous little pricks who can't write 'bum' on a wall are packing them in in droves at the Royal Court. Can you imagine how that makes me feel? It's a total humiliation.

(*Of the script.*) And this could turn things round for me. It's bold. It's honest. When did I ever show two men kissing before? That means a lot to me. It makes me proud. They can hate it if they like, but they *cannot* say...

(Of the script again.) ... that *this* was written by a piss-elegant old queen who's too frightened to tell the truth about himself.

CEDRIC. Then why are you behaving like one?

TERRY. What?

CEDRIC. You heard me.

Pause.

Terry, why don't you simply tell me what you want?

TERRY. Well, it would break my heart not to see this play. But I'd rather it wasn't made.

CEDRIC. Then why did you write it?

TERRY. I don't know.

CEDRIC. You signed a contract!

Strings of lanterns start descending for the ball, while STEWARDS *begin arranging the festivities on deck.* CEDRIC *continues oblivious.*

We paid you four thousand pounds! *Four thousand smackers!* Do you know what it took to get you that? I had to get down on my *knees.* I had to *grovel.* You haven't offered to pay it back, I notice. Oh no, I forgot, you've got three houses.

TERRY. Don't be a bastard!

CEDRIC. If you want me to go crawling back to those disgusting little toads on the sixth floor and say, 'Oh, ever so sorry, chaps, Sir Terence Rattigan's in a blue funk about his play so our money's gone down the toilet,' then I want you to tell me *now.* I mean *tonight.* No *sodding about.* Have you got that? Call me at home.

He's about to go.

I hate to bully you. But I've got too much respect for you to allow you to make such a twat of yourself. Goodnight.

As CEDRIC *goes, the ship's deck is transformed into the site of the ball, now at its height. It's night and there's a full moon. Everyone is there, except for* NIJINSKY *and* ROMOLA, *and all are in fancy dress, dancing ragtime.*

ROMOLA *enters dressed as a boy in evening dress. She looks terrific.* GUNZBURG, *who is dressed as… Mephistopheles? A vampyr? Something self-dramatisingly sinister, anyway… sidles up to her.*

GUNZBURG. Mademoiselle looks perfect.

ROMOLA. I don't think he'll like it much… unless his taste is for very *plain* boys with bulges in all the wrong places.

NIJINSKY *can be seen approaching. He is dressed in a dinner jacket, so that his and* ROMOLA*'s dress is practically identical.*

GUNZBURG (*hissing*). He's here!

NIJINSKY *is at the table.*

May I present Mademoiselle Romola de Pulzky?

NIJINSKY *bows gravely.*

NIJINSKY. *O, u Vas zamechatielnyi kostum!*

ROMOLA *is at a loss.*

GUNZBURG (*translates*). May I congratulate you on your stylish costume?

ROMOLA. *Tetszik Maganak?*

GUNZBURG (*translates*). Do you like it?

NIJINSKY. *Da. U arteesta nie dolzhno byt' pola.*

GUNZBURG. I do. An artist should be without gender.

ROMOLA (*puzzled*). *Koszonom*, Monsieur Nijinsky

GUNZBURG (*translates*). Thank you, Monsieur Nijinsky.

NIJINSKY. *Zoveete menya Vaslav, pozhalujsta.*

GUNZBURG. Call me Vaslav, please.

ROMOLA. Vaslav.

NIJINSKY. *A chto za moozyku oni igrayut?*

GUNZBURG (*translates*). What is this music they are playing?

ROMOLA. *Fez egy uj tanc, tangonak hivyak.*

GUNZBURG (*translates*). It is a new dance called the tango.

NIJINSKY. *Boodete li Vy tak dobry naucheet' menya?*

i.e. 'Would you be kind enough to teach it to me?' But no translation is necessary: he holds out his arms in invitation. They begin to dance a tango. ROMOLA *is expert.* NIJINSKY *has never danced it before, and perhaps he's never danced at a party at all, so at first he looks over-balletic and, paradoxically, rather clumsy; it's like Kiri Te Kanawa singing* West Side Story. *But, under* ROMOLA*'s influence – because she's confident and laughing now – he loosens up. They soon look a perfect team; they move together, they seem to read each other's thoughts.*

Later, the two of them are dancing together on a deserted dance floor. The music comes to an end. They kiss.

Dissolve to the same night, now very late. Full moon. A light flares in the darkness: it's GUNZBURG, *drawing on his cigarette.* NIJINSKY *appears out of the darkness.*

GUNZBURG. Well?

NIJINSKY. I want to marry her. I believe that God, too, wants me to marry her. But it will break Sergei Pavlovich's heart.

GUNZBURG. Not at all, dear friend. He'll be delighted. A marriage that means nothing to you, will free you both from any hint of scandal.

NIJINSKY (*angrily*). That means nothing? How can you say that? A marriage is a holy sacrament. One swears to it before God. It must mean *everything*.

GUNZBURG *looks at him thoughtfully.*

GUNZBURG. I understand you now.

NIJINSKY. Will you do me a kindness? Ask her to marry me. I can't do it.

ROMOLA appears in the darkness.

ROMOLA (*calls*). Vaslav?

NIJINSKY steps back into the darkness. ROMOLA steps forward to GUNZBURG.

GUNZBURG. Mademoiselle?

ROMOLA. Have you seen him?

GUNZBURG. Yes, only a moment ago. He entrusted me with a task.

ROMOLA. What is it?

GUNZBURG. I am to ask you, on his behalf, for your hand in marriage.

There is a long pause. ROMOLA puts her hands to her cheeks.

ROMOLA. How *can* you? Oh, how *can* you be so unkind? So it was all a joke?

She is crying.

GUNZBURG. No, let me explain...!

NIJINSKY steps out of the darkness. He signals to GUNZBURG, who steps into the darkness and out of sight.

NIJINSKY. Romola...

He searches for a way to start. It's difficult. He indicates 'talk'.

Vy govoreete po russki? [Do you speak Russian?]

He shakes his head questioningly. She shakes hers.

ROMOLA. *Russki, nem. Beszél Magyarul?* [No. Do you speak Hungarian?]

NIJINSKY. *Magyarul...?*

He gets it and smiles.

Hungarian!

ROMOLA (*hopefully*). *Igen!* [Yes!]

He shakes his head.

NIJINSKY. *Niet. A vy govoreete po polski?* [No. Do you speak Polish?]

ROMOLA, *near to tears, shakes her head.*

ROMOLA. *Polski nem non plus.*

She has an idea.

(*Hopefully.*) Ah! *Parlez-vous Français?*

He frowns.

NIJINSKY. *Oui, un… peu.*

Pause.

ROMOLA. *Donc…*

NIJINSKY. Romola…

ROMOLA. *Oui?*

NIJINSKY. *C'est… vrai que le Baron… vous a dit. Vous comprenez?*

ROMOLA *nods, her heart in her mouth.*

ROMOLA. *Oui, je comprends.*

NIJINSKY. *Voulez-vous…?*

ROMOLA. *Voulez-vous…?*

NIJINSKY. … *vous et moi…?*

ROMOLA. *Vous et moi…?*

He gives up. Signals, in classic ballet-mime, 'heart', 'your beautiful face', 'marry me', 'my kingdom will be yours'. ROMOLA nods. He takes a ring off his finger, fits it on hers. GUNZBURG appears out of the darkness.

GUNZBURG (*quietly to* ROMOLA). He will buy you a better one in Buenos Aires.

Lights focus down to an iris on NIJINSKY *and* ROMOLA, *and climactic music swells accordingly.*

But it stops abruptly, and the silence is broken by a huge, amplified roar of pain and fury. It's DIAGHILEV *who has uttered it. We see him doing so again, collapsed prostrate on to the floor.* BAKST *and* GRIGORIEV *watch him, alarmed.* BAKST *has a newspaper in his hand.*

DIAGHILEV (*commanding him*). Read it again.

BAKST (*reads*). 'Vaslav Nijinsky has made some astonishing leaps in his day, but none so astounding as the one he made yesterday in Buenos Aires, when he married an unknown Hungarian heiress...'

DIAGHILEV (*violently*). Stop it! Burn it!

BAKST *crumples the newspaper.*

BAKST. It won't burn the fact.

DIAGHILEV. The fact, my friends, is that the Diaghilev Ballet is dead. I'll try to pay you for the work you have done. You can all go back to Russia, or wherever it is you go when you're not working for me. Goodbye, gentlemen.

The others go. DIAGHILEV *remains crouched on the floor.* TERRY *refers to his script.*

TERRY (*to* DIAGHILEV). For the next three days you disappear from sight.

DIAGHILEV. True!

TERRY. Benois finds you at last in a brothel, sleeping it off in bed with two French rent boys.

DIAGHILEV. True! All true!

TERRY. He informs you that he, Bakst and Stravinsky have decided to stay in Paris and offer their work to the Paris Opera...

DIAGHILEV. The Paris Opera! Those *gangsters*! That *repulsive* audience! Are they *out of their minds*?

TERRY.... and the Diaghilev Ballet is promptly reassembled.

DIAGHILEV. Of course it is reassembled! Should I allow the greatest artistic movement of the twentieth century to be destroyed by a Polish potato farmer? I will pursue him to the ends of the earth! I will annihilate him!

DIAGHILEV stays in place, as NIJINSKY and ROMOLA arrive in Budapest followed by PORTERS carrying luggage. ROMOLA is heavily pregnant. With them is ROMOLA's mother, EMILIA MARKUS, a distinguished Hungarian actress in the Bernhardt style. They are met by a flurry of NEWSPAPER REPORTERS and PHOTOGRAPHERS. A press conference is under way.

FIRST REPORTER. Madame Nijinsky... when did you arrive in Budapest?

ROMOLA. This morning.

FIRST REPORTER. And why are you here?

EMILIA. Well, obviously to bring her husband to meet his mother-in-law.

ROMOLA. And also to have my baby here.

SECOND REPORTER. When is the baby due?

ROMOLA. Very soon.

THIRD REPORTER (*to* NIJINSKY). Mr Nijinsky, do you want a boy or a girl?

ROMOLA. A girl, of course, and she'll be the greatest actress in the world.

THIRD REPORTER. Taking after her grandmother?

EMILIA. How kind you are! We hope, of course, that she will make her name in the theatre, just like myself.

There is a FOURTH REPORTER lingering in the shadows. Meanwhile, the press conference continues, with EMILIA grabbing most of the attention and NIJINSKY *looking acutely ill at ease.*

FIRST REPORTER. If it's a boy, he could be a dancer like his father.

ROMOLA. He could never be a dancer like his father.

EMILIA. Besides, a male dancer... with, of course, one great exception...

She smiles politely at NIJINSKY, *who remains stony-faced.*

...is just a little...

She makes an expressive gesture.

...you know what I mean.

NIJINSKY (*pleading*). Please, can we finish?

EMILIA. Oh, but I'm sure these ladies and gentlemen have many more questions.

ROMOLA (*looking anxiously at* NIJINSKY). Mother, that's enough. Vaslav is tired.

EMILIA *goes out with the* REPORTERS.

EMILIA (*announcing*). Now don't forget: my next role in Budapest will be *Phèdre*. Yes, the Sarah Bernhardt version.

NIJINSKY *sits down heavily, holding his head.*

ROMOLA. Is it your headache?

He nods.

Stay there and I'll fetch your medicine.

She goes out. Only the FOURTH REPORTER *remains. He now approaches* NIJINSKY.

FOURTH REPORTER. Monsieur Nijinsky...

NIJINSKY. Yes?

FOURTH REPORTER. ...I am from *The Times* of London.

NIJINSKY. Go on?

FOURTH REPORTER. I'm sorry to disturb you when you are not feeling well, but no one has asked you the most important question of all. Is it true, as rumoured in London, that you recently sent a telegram to Diaghilev telling him that, after your child is born, you will be willing to continue to work for him?

NIJINSKY *looks at him, awakened as if meeting an undiscovered friend.*

NIJINSKY. Oh. Yes, that is true.

DIAGHILEV, *still spread out on the floor, unfolds the telegram, screws in his monocle and reads it.*

FOURTH REPORTER. Have you had his reply?

NIJINSKY. No, we've been travelling.

FOURTH REPORTER. Well, the story was published in St Petersburg this morning.

NIJINSKY. What does it say?

FOURTH REPORTER. Read for yourself.

He hands NIJINSKY *a Russian newspaper.* GRIGORIEV *approaches* DIAGHILEV, *as one who has been summoned.* DIAGHILEV *stands.*

DIAGHILEV. Grigoriev, dear friend, I have received this telegram from Nijinsky.

He takes off his monocle, places the telegram down and, rather elaborately, puts the palm of his hand over it. (GRIGORIEV *wrote later: 'This is what he always did with any communication that annoyed him.'*)

This is my answer.

GRIGORIEV *takes out a pen and notebook.* NIJINSKY *reads while* DIAGHILEV *dictates. It's clear that the exercise gives him malicious pleasure.*

In reply to your telegram, I wish to inform you of the following. Monsieur Diaghilev…

GRIGORIEV *looks up in surprise.*

...Monsieur Diaghilev considers that by missing a performance on the recent South American tour, you are in breach of contract. He will not therefore require your further services. Signed: Sergei Grigoriev, General Manager, the Diaghilev Company.

(*To* GRIGORIEV.) Send it.

GRIGORIEV *is shocked.*

GRIGORIEV. Signed by me?

DIAGHILEV. Exactly!

He chuckles. GRIGORIEV *goes.* DIAGHILEV *brings out, or finds, a mirror. Brushes his hair with black dye and applies a little discreet make-up to his face.* NIJINSKY *stays where he is, motionless with shock.*

FOURTH REPORTER. Did you miss a performance in South America?

NIJINSKY (*whispering*). Just one. My wedding night.

ROMOLA *appears, stirring his glass of medicine.* NIJINSKY *takes the glass and violently hurls it out of sight.*

(*Spitting out the words.*) You can publish this, Mr Reporter from *The Times.* I intend to sue Monsieur Diaghilev for every franc he owes me. And you may also publish this: I, Vaslav Nijinsky, will never work for Sergei... Pavlovich... Diaghilev again.

FOURTH REPORTER. You will be working, then, for Baron de Gunzburg?

NIJINSKY. Why do you ask me *that*?

FOURTH REPORTER. Because he has announced the formation of his own ballet company, and that you are to be his principal dancer.

NIJINSKY. I will dance for no one, Monsieur... if not for Diaghilev. Nobody in the world. Print that please.

FOURTH REPORTER. Thank you, Monsieur.

He folds his notebook and goes.

NIJINSKY (*whispering*). God, why did you do this? What have I done to you?

ROMOLA. But, Vaslav… every company in the world will want you now.

NIJINSKY. That is no use to me. They will want me to do my *entrechat-dix*. I can't dance like that any more. I'm a dancer of the future. I am a maker of dance. It was Sergei Pavlovich who made me that. Now that I've lost him, I have nothing.

He closes his eyes.

I close my eyes and even the darkness is empty. All I can see is circles. Always circles… One vast circle, the whole of the universe, on fire…

ROMOLA *leads him out as a short, striking-looking boy of eighteen approaches* DIAGHILEV*'s presence. This is* LEONID MASSINE.

MASSINE. Maître Diaghilev?

DIAGHILEV *smuggles away his hair dye and make-up and affects surprise.*

DIAGHILEV. Who are you?

MASSINE (*nervously*). I am the dancer you saw at the Bolshoi last night. You told me to come and see you at ten o'clock this morning. Unhappily it is now nearly two and I must go and catch my train back to Moscow. It's a long journey, as you know…

DIAGHILEV. Sit down.

MASSINE. But… my train…

DIAGHILEV. There are always others.

MASSINE. Not until tomorrow.

DIAGHILEV. Well then, you must stay the night in St Petersburg, mustn't you?

MASSINE. But my mother…

DIAGHILEV. I shall send her a telegram to say that you will be in my personal care tonight, which will, of course, reassure her.

He pushes the reluctant boy into a chair.

How old are you?

MASSINE. Eighteen.

DIAGHILEV. Good… not too old to become a great dancer. Though at the moment, I must note that you are disconcertingly short offstage, your legs are bandy and, judging by last night's performance, you don't even dance very well.

MASSINE. But, Maître Diaghilev, I have decided to become an actor.

DIAGHILEV. Very wise. Dancing is a horrible life. Endless drudgery, too much discipline, strict training. I would hate it for myself.

He gets up to pour himself another vodka.

Nevertheless, you are going to be a dancer… and very likely the greatest dancer in the world.

MASSINE. Bar one?

DIAGHILEV, *only momentarily disconcerted, laughs and raises his glass.*

DIAGHILEV. Bar one! Bravo! Something tells me that you and I are going to understand each other very well, my dear… what is your name again?

MASSINE. Myasin. Leonid Myasin.

DIAGHILEV. Leonid I will allow you. But as for 'Myasin'… it has no style, it has no *flourish*. You will be Leonid… Massine. Yes, that's an excellent name for a dancer.

MASSINE. But I'm going to be an actor!

DIAGHILEV. We'll see how you feel about that in the morning, shall we? Meanwhile, I recommend this vodka. It comes from the Kaiser's cellar… so much better than the Tsar's.

As they go out, NIJINSKY *appears. He no longer wears the natty clothes he wore before. His clothes now are homespun Tolstoyan Russian. A wooden cross hangs around his neck. He starts drawing, either on sheets of paper, or on the walls. Quickly it becomes apparent that he's drawing circles, more and more until they surround the action.*

ROMOLA *wheels on a pram.* EMILIA *approaches her with determination.*

EMILIA. Romola, I'm having no more of this. You must get a divorce at once.

ROMOLA (*mildly*). On what grounds?

She sits and takes out her knitting.

EMILIA. That your husband is an enemy alien.

ROMOLA. If *he* is an alien, then so am I.

EMILIA. Only because he's made you one. The state will very readily grant a divorce in a case like this…

ROMOLA. And the Church?

EMILIA. How does the Church come into it?

ROMOLA. At my wedding, I swore a vow. I'm not going to break it now, or ever.

EMILIA. Are *you* infected with his madness? Because he *is* mad.

ROMOLA. He is *what*?

EMILIA. He's a religious maniac. Surely you realise that? The police found him dancing in an empty church…

ROMOLA. He was practising!

EMILIA. … and now he's gone upstairs to pray for the war to end. To *pray*! He can't support you any more, because he's got no money left.

ROMOLA *gets up and faces her mother. We see a girl who has very quickly developed from a flirtatious, self-centred little gadabout, into a young woman of emerging character, maturity and understanding. Also possessed of a certain fatalism, for she must know, by now, something of the 'fatal' truth.*

ROMOLA. Mother, you can throw us out if that's what you want to do. But you will never separate me from Vaslav. Nothing can. 'Till death do us part...' Remember?

EMILIA. Death? Or Diaghilev?

ROMOLA (*lightly*). Oh, death, I think.

She looks at the pram.

Little Kyra needs the shade. Forgive me, Mother. I'll see you at lunch, won't I?

EMILIA *leaves.* ROMOLA *stays, absorbed in her baby.* NIJINSKY *stays, still drawing, while...*

...DIAGHILEV *arrives in New York, accompanied by* PORTERS. *Popular music is heard as if backstage: early Irving Berlin or something like that. A couple of* CHORUS GIRLS *dash past in costume, laughing.* DIAGHILEV *views them with some disdain.* OTTO KAHN, *a hard-headed impresario, enters, carrying a large account book.*

DIAGHILEV. My dear Otto, there is *no* need whatsoever to apologise for keeping me waiting for at least twenty minutes...

KAHN. I'm not going to. I was taking a look at these figures.

DIAGHILEV. Figures are seldom my concern.

KAHN. Well, they should be. Do you know the loss your ballet company is taking at the Century Theatre?

DIAGHILEV. Can I help it if your New York audiences are barbarians?

KAHN. They may be barbarians, but they know when they're being taken for a ride.

DIAGHILEV. A *ride*? In my country, that remark would cause a duel and I would kill you. Here, in this preposterous city, shadowed by concrete Towers of Babel, I can only ask, 'What kind of ride?'

KAHN. You promised me ballet stars…

DIAGHILEV. … and you promised me the Metropolitan Opera House, where the box-office takings are stupendous!

KAHN. You can have the Metropolitan on one condition. That you get me Nijinsky.

DIAGHILEV. But I have brought you Fokine!

KAHN. There's just one problem with Fokine. Nobody's heard of him and nobody cares.

DIAGHILEV. Well, Nijinsky can't come to New York. He is interned in Hungary.

KAHN. Not any longer. I have a contact in the State Department who has gotten him and his family into Switzerland. He's only waiting for a cable. He can be here in three weeks.

DIAGHILEV. I'm overjoyed. Send him a cable and give him a job.

KAHN. No, the cable must come from you. He insists on that.

DIAGHILEV. I hate to doubt your word, my dear Mr Kahn, but he has told the world that he will never work for me again.

KAHN. He's told my contact that he will, as long as you ask him… What did he say?

He consults a note. ROMOLA *looks up from the pram to dictate to* NIJINSKY, *who repeats her words…*

ROMOLA. 'With a full, honest and loving heart.'

DIAGHILEV. He never did learn to express himself properly. I tried very hard to educate him, but Poles will be Poles. Will he have that woman with him?

KAHN. Do you mean Madame Nijinsky?

DIAGHILEV. That was the person I referred to.

KAHN. He won't travel without her. Or his child.

DIAGHILEV. *His* child? Parthenogenesis is the accepted view. I can have the Metropolitan, did you say? Is that a promise?

KAHN *nods and hands him a telegram form.* DIAGHILEV *takes out his pen and begins to write:*

'Beloved Vaslav...'

NIJINSKY *responds as though he's heard these words. At this point we need a big table from somewhere; the two antagonists position themselves at opposite ends of it.* DIAGHILEV *lights a cigar. They are acutely aware of each other, but they resist any kind of overt acknowledgment.*

They are joined at the table by KAHN, GRIGORIEV *and two* LAWYERS. *The scene should appear to us as it does to the two ex-lovers: that nobody in the room is entirely real except for them.*

ROMOLA *becomes aware of the circles that* NIJINSKY *has been drawing. She moves up to them, touches them, studies them for meaning.*

KAHN (*addressing the two* LAWYERS). Let me get this straight. Your client, Mr Nijinsky, agrees to give a further eleven performances at the Metropolitan...

LAWYER 1.... provided that Mr Diaghilev pays him his arrears of pay over the last seven years.

KAHN (*impatiently*). Not all his arrears! Jesus Christ, that's impossible! We agreed the figure at three thousand dollars a performance, taken out of receipts...

LAWYER 2.... but paid in cash before each performance by Mr Diaghilev or his agent.

DIAGHILEV (*his face a mask*). My agent.

KAHN. Now, as for the tour...

LAWYER 2. ... Mr Nijinsky agrees to undertake the tour provided that...

He looks at a document that seems to shock even him.

My God!... That Mr Diaghilev hands over the entire artistic direction to Mr Nijinsky and leaves the United States until Mr Nijinsky has returned to Switzerland.

DIAGHILEV. I agree.

KAHN. You *do*?

DIAGHILEV *shrugs*.

DIAGHILEV. I have work to do in Europe, and I am only too happy to put three thousand miles between myself and Monsieur Nijinsky. Well, gentlemen, if that is all our business...

The LAWYERS *circulate documents around the table. They are complex documents with signatures required on many pages.* DIAGHILEV, NIJINSKY *and* KAHN *all sign. Meanwhile:*

TERRY, *alongside the others at the conference table, feverishly types, or bashes out, the following on a portable typewriter. The text is projected in typewriter font. Or he speaks it... Or it's projected, with him speaking the passages he especially wants to emphasise.*

TERRY. 'Author's note: Osborne and Pinter don't write these, but Graham Greene, J.B. Priestley and I do. You can disregard them if you wish, or you can regard them and perhaps find them of some help.

This scene is the last *explicit* encounter between the two most famous lovers since Romeo and Juliet... "notorious", if you like to change the epithet to please your vicar...

... and the author, in a long and turbulent career, has never *funked* a scene where two leading characters face each other in conflict, otherwise known as a "scène à faire". He's written many of those, and has usually been criticised for

doing so. The following scene is the "scène à faire" of the
present screenplay.

He takes a swig of J&B.

It contains no angry denunciations, no screams of abuse, no
physical violence. This is because, in my experience, as long
as such lively events are taking place, there is always the
chance that love will be rekindled. It is only in the cold, grey
dawn of disappointment, that love finally dies. Hence the tone
and brevity of what I've written. If any of you can think up a
better scene, I will welcome your suggestions... but I happen
to think that *this* is the best one, or I wouldn't have written it.'

*He rips the paper out of the typewriter and places it in his
script. The signing of contracts is complete.* NIJINSKY *puts
down his pen and looks* DIAGHILEV *in the eye.* TERRY
*watches them at close hand, as though a part of the scene.
He is greatly, deeply moved.*

NIJINSKY (*quietly*). Why are you happy to put three thousand
miles between us?

*We sense his hurt; it's clear that the harsh conditions of the
contract were only a way of reaching through*
DIAGHILEV's *defences.*

DIAGHILEV. You know why.

NIJINSKY. I don't, Sergei Pavlovich. I really don't. I came here
expecting... hoping...

DIAGHILEV (*harshly*).... that I would have forgotten your
broken vow?

NIJINSKY (*puzzled*). My vow?

DIAGHILEV. You *have* forgotten it. Interesting.

TERRY (*mutters*). Bastard.

DIAGHILEV. It was a vow that you made one night in Paris.
You said you would make it on your mother's head, and I
asked you to make it to your own head. I hope that your God
doesn't exact his full price. It was a head I treasured. Once.

He nods curtly to KAHN *and the* LAWYERS *and leaves the room. The* LAWYERS *collect papers.* NIJINSKY *collapses into a chair, his face blank. After a moment, he begins to mutter inaudibly and to cross himself.*

LAWYER 1 (*quietly to the* LAWYER 2). What's he saying?

LAWYER 2. A prayer, I think.

LAWYER 1. I would guess that he needs to say quite a few of those.

LAWYER 2. And the other one even more.

ROMOLA *leaves the drawn circles, brings one of the drawings with her, and hands it to a young doctor,* DR FRENKEL.

ROMOLA. But, Dr Frenkel, I was only looking at these drawings of his. But it made him angry. That's when he attacked me. Then moments later, he'd forgotten all about it.

DR FRENKEL. I'm not surprised. When I saw him in December for his headaches, I was quite certain that he was on the way to a mental breakdown.

ROMOLA. A breakdown can be temporary, can't it?

DR FRENKEL. Of course it can. But for the time being, I'm quite sure that he would be better off in a sanatorium. Now, very fortunately, a Professor Bleuler is arriving here in St Moritz for a conference. You have heard of him?

ROMOLA *shakes her head.*

He is the greatest expert in the world on mental disorders. He has artistic tastes, and will doubtless be an admirer of your husband. I'm quite sure that he will be able to help.

ROMOLA. Vatzka will never see him if he thinks that he's a doctor.

DR FRENKEL. Then we must think up some little subterfuge. Don't despair. These things are curable.

They go out as:

DIAGHILEV. So you grew to like her in the end?

TERRY. I did. She was silly and flighty to start with, but then something else took over and she became quite admirable. She was incredibly loyal to him.

DIAGHILEV. Doesn't it strike you as ironic that both you and I fought her for the possession of Nijinsky?

TERRY. Except that you didn't fight.

DIAGHILEV. I didn't?

TERRY. You gave in. That's what's so odd. You sacked him. You insulted him. You made it impossible for him to come back to you. And I can't help feeling there's something deeply unconvincing about the Baron who did the matchmaking. Was he acting for himself? Or was he really acting for you?

DIAGHILEV (*evasively*). He may have known what it was I wanted.

TERRY. So all that howling and hysteria when Nijinsky and Romola married... was it sincere?

DIAGHILEV. I am not English! I don't hide my emotions! I was heartbroken! But I am also a showman. How could I afford a choreographer whose dances nobody liked?

TERRY. That was the reason?

DIAGHILEV. Besides, there's a limit to how long one man can sustain erotic interest in another.

TERRY. So you passed him on to Romola without either of them knowing that's what you'd done?

DIAGHILEV. A good writer like you are ought to know that nothing is ever so simple.

TERRY *stares at him.*

TERRY. Do you think I'm a good writer?

DIAGHILEV. You are a *very* good writer. But imagine… if you
had written in flaming colours, like a setting by Bakst or
Benois. Or if your characters spoke to the visceral pulse of
Stravinsky, and not Puccini. Do you see what I'm saying, my
friend? If I had been your producer, you would have been
more than a very good writer. You would have been a great
writer, and you would have written your great play.

TERRY. I doubt it.

(Of the script.) But I'm quite sure that's why I wrote about
you in this.

DIAGHILEV. Will you let Romola kill it?

TERRY. Oh yes.

DIAGHILEV. But that's absurd! Your *art* is the only thing that
should matter to you. What are you frightened of? Vaslav
and I destroyed entire hotel suites with the ardour of our
lovemaking! So they put a few extra francs on the bill. No
shame! No blushes! You have two years left to live, you say.
Live them honestly!

DIAGHILEV *indicates the telephone.*

There is the telephone. Use it.

TERRY *lifts the receiver. As he's dialling, he sees* ROMOLA
and NIJINSKY *appear from the opposite side to* DR
FRENKEL. ROMOLA *is limping.*

TERRY. They're here.

He places his finger on the telephone rest.

DIAGHILEV. She's pretending she's hurt her leg. Frenkel was
her lover, by the way. That's what drove Vatzka mad.

TERRY. In your opinion.

DIAGHILEV. Whose else matters?

And we focus down to DR FRENKEL'*s surgery.*

DR FRENKEL. Madame Nijinsky, how very nice to see you
again. I hope it's nothing serious.

ROMOLA. Just a sore ankle. I was foolish enough to fall down some stairs.

DR FRENKEL. A common accident. Monsieur Nijinsky, you look splendid. It was good of you to accompany Madame to my surgery. Do sit down.

He opens the door of the consulting room. ROMOLA *goes in and* DR FRENKEL *follows her. Another door opens and an elderly man comes in.*

BLEULER. Oh, forgive me. I am a house guest here, and I've lost my way.

DIAGHILEV. The Professor. What a fake!

BLEULER. Are you waiting to see Dr Frenkel?

NIJINSKY. No, my wife is with him.

BLEULER. Then perhaps I might keep you company?

NIJINSKY *is uneasy.*

NIJINSKY. Are you a doctor?

BLEULER. No, I'm here for the music festival.

(*Overdoing it.*) Good Lord! Aren't you... could you be... the great Vaslav Nijinsky?

NIJINSKY *nods.*

This is indeed a privilege. I have seen you dance so many times, and always with delight.

NIJINSKY. Thank you.

BLEULER. Tell me, how do you execute that great leap in *Spectre de la Rose*, where you seem to stop in mid-air and then go higher?

NIJINSKY. I leap as high as I can – and then I wait for God to take me higher. And he always does. All things are possible when God is in you. Faith can make a man into God.

DIAGHILEV. Which, in the Professor's eyes, is proof of madness.

BLEULER. Any man?

NIJINSKY. Not any man, no. Only the truly chosen. Only one man.

BLEULER. But surely only one man has been God?

NIJINSKY. If one man, why not another? Didn't He say He would come again?

BLEULER. Indeed, so I believe. Forgive me for being so personal, but are your eyes green, or is that just an illusion?

He comes closer and stares for quite a long time into NIJINSKY*'s eyes.*

An illusion. They are grey. Do forgive my silly questions. You see, I am *such* an admirer of yours. You were saying, just now, about the 'truly chosen' and the 'Godhead'. That is a fascinating concept...

ROMOLA *and* DR FRENKEL *look round the door in* Commedia dell'Arte *'eavesdropping' style.*

ROMOLA. What is to be the sign?

DR FRENKEL. A recording of Caruso.

BLEULER *drops the needle on a Caruso record.* DR FRENKEL *and* ROMOLA *enter.*

Monsieur Nijinsky, your wife is fine! Just a little chip off the bone, which will mend of its own accord.

(*To* BLEULER.) Professor Bleuler! You have met our distinguished friend?

BLEULER. We have had a delightful conversation.

DR FRENKEL. Monsieur Nijinsky, I want to try a new prescription for those headaches of yours. Will you step into the consulting room for a moment?

NIJINSKY *looks impassively at* ROMOLA.

NIJINSKY (*quietly, leaning forward*). Little wife, you have brought me my death warrant.

He follows DR FRENKEL *into the consulting room, leaving* ROMOLA *with* BLEULER, *who takes the needle off the record.*

ROMOLA. Well?

BLEULER. Madame Nijinsky, there is no good way to say this. He is insane.

ROMOLA. Incurably?

BLEULER. There's no cure for schizophrenia. Your husband is a menace not only to society, but to you and your child. You must abandon him absolutely.

ROMOLA (*quite lightly*). Oh, I could never do that. If he's a menace to other people then, of course, he must... go to some safer place. But I must be with him... always... till he dies.

BLEULER. Do you realise what this would mean for you? It will be a life of misery.

ROMOLA. It won't be what I imagined, but it's the only life I could live. *With* him.

BLEULER (*with a sigh*). Very well. You had better go home now and pack his things.

He has scribbled an address on a piece of paper. Now he gives it to her.

Bring them tomorrow morning to this address. He will be taken there separately.

ROMOLA. He will lock himself in his room at home.

BLEULER. The police will break it down. If he is well enough after the shock of his removal, you may be allowed to see him.

ROMOLA (*of the address*). What is this place?

BLEULER. It's a secure surrounding. If he responds to treatment, we can move him. You are very brave.

ROMOLA. Not brave at all… just… well… what you called me… twice or even three times… I can't remember… Madame Nijinsky… and after all, that's what I am.

They go out. TERRY *looks at the telephone.*

DIAGHILEV. Tell your producer that the play will go ahead.

TERRY. I can't. You see…

Pause.

… if I write a play, I'm not just saying the things that I want to say. I'm also saying the things that I want to hide. My bitterness or my weakness or my absurd infatuations and betrayals or my, my queerness, even. I'm not saying my women are all men, or any of that rubbish. It makes me terribly angry when people say that. My women are women, and they're bloody well-written ones. But my queerness is there all the time, only it's under the surface. If I became… *officially* a queer, if I had a big sign saying 'queer' hanging over my head, then there'd be *nothing* under the surface. It would all be obvious. All banality. I'd be a preacher. That's not acceptable.

He's dialling.

Let me do this quickly.

The call is answered.

Hello, is Cedric home yet? Could I speak to him?

POLICE *enter at speed and attack a door with axes. It collapses in splinters. They dive in and pull* NIJINSKY *out from his hiding place.* NURSES *strap him into a straitjacket. He utters a piercing scream of fear and fury. He struggles. As they carry him away:*

Cedric, it's me. I'm sorry I was so silly this afternoon. (*Pause.*) Hang on, hang on. I've had a wonderful idea. I want you to hold back on the play for now. I want you to get on with the Shakespeares and do my play afterwards. Then you can tell your money-men that my show has simply been postponed, and there'll be no comeback. (*Pause.*) No, I don't mind waiting. (*Pause.*) Three years, I know, you told me, and

Romola's sure to be dead by then, she's really tottery, I'd give her a year. And then I'll come to the shooting whenever you like. I'll poke my nose into the casting, I'll rewrite whatever you want me to...

He's crying.

... we'll sit side by side in the viewing room, and I'll be prouder and happier than I've been in all my life. I know how hard it will be for you to get this through the system, but... (*Pause.*) Oh, will you? Thank you. Thank you. (*Pause.*) And to you.

He replaces the receiver.

DIAGHILEV. You said it would break your heart if you didn't see it.

TERRY. I expect it will.

There's a burst of music, and we're in a theatre watching the final moment of Petrouschka: *Petrouschka* (*or his ghost*) *appears over the top of the set with frantic waving hands, and then falls, apparently lifeless again, with swinging hands over the edge of the booth.*

The ballet is over.

TANNOY VOICE. All company to stay onstage, please.

And the CAST *gathers onstage.*

DANCER 1. I wonder who it is? Is it the French President?

DANCER 2. Oh, probably just another exiled Grand Duke.

DANCER 3. But didn't you see how Karsavina bowed to the Royal Box? Practically to the ground.

GRIGORIEV *appears.*

GRIGORIEV. Members of the company, most of you know that Vaslav Nijinsky has been in a nursing home for the last four years. I can tell you now that Maître Diaghilev invited him to see this performance of *Petrouschka*, in the hope that it will help his recovery. He will be here in a moment.

They wait. NIJINSKY, *held on one side by a smiling*
ROMOLA, *on the other by an equally smiling*
DIAGHILEV, *walks slowly on to be greeted by applause*
from the whole company. His face is blank, his eyes are
vacant. The impression is of a puppet held by two
puppeteers.

He shuffles along the line of DANCERS, *putting his hand*
out obediently to be shaken when told. He reaches to the
'Petrouschka' DANCER *and stares at him as though*
searching for something irretrievably lost. Next he faces
KARSAVINA, *and smiles at her with seeming recognition.*

KARSAVINA (*kissing him*). Vatzka… my darling Vatzka.

He accepts the embrace but then shuffles down the line; he
didn't, after all, know who she was. DIAGHILEV *places an*
arm around NIJINSKY's *shoulder.*

DIAGHILEV. Goodbye, my Vatzka. Go with God.

NIJINSKY. With God.

He shuffles away, his eyes on DIAGHILEV's, *and*
DIAGHILEV's *on his, until he is out of sight.* KARSAVINA
embraces ROMOLA.

KARSAVINA. My darling… I'm so sorry.

ROMOLA. Don't pity me. I thank God that he let me live in
this century, when I could see Nijinsky dance.

She moves on.

GRIGORIEV (*off*). Thank you, ladies and gentlemen. The call
tomorrow is barre at eleven a.m. with Maestro Cecchetti.
Sylphides principals at one, corps at two-thirty. Madame
Karsavina and Monsieur Bolm at three-thirty for *Spectre de*
la Rose…

The announcement dies away. DIAGHILEV *and the*
DANCERS *have dissolved and left.* TERRY *is alone. The*
lights come up on his suite. DONALD *is standing in the*
middle of the room.

TERRY. Hello?

DONALD. It's Donald, Sir Terence. I came to turn down your bed.

TERRY. Oh, thank you.

He rises and totters.

DONALD. Shall I help you, sir?

He supports him, but TERRY *stumbles, nearly collapses.*

TERRY. I don't think I'm going to make it. Why don't you chuck a blanket or two on the sofa? I'll sleep on that.

DONALD. Are you sure about that, sir?

TERRY. I'm sure.

He sits somewhere, takes off his shoes and jacket.

Oh, by the way. I need someone to book me a cab to Lord's in the morning.

DONALD. I'll do that, sir.

TERRY. Thank you.

DONALD *collects sheets and blankets.*

DONALD. It's England versus India, isn't it, sir? I wish I was going myself. We've got a radio down in the kitchen. I'll be listening in. We all of us will.

TERRY. Do you play?

DONALD. I certainly do, sir.

He lays down a sheet. TERRY *lies on it.*

How will that be for you, sir? Not too untidy?

TERRY. It'll be fine.

DONALD *covers him with a sheet and blanket.*

DONALD. Bishan Bedi ought to be nigh unplayable after all this rain, sir.

TERRY. I'm afraid he will be.

DONALD. What's that blue thing that he wears on his head?

TERRY. It's called a patka.

> DONALD *turns away, perhaps to take a blanket back to the bedroom.* TERRY, *quickly and silently, performs the classical gestures: 'your beautiful face', 'I love you', 'all this will be yours'.*

> DONALD *turns back with no idea of what's just happened.*

DONALD. What, sir?

TERRY. Are *you* a bowler?

DONALD. Mostly, sir. I used to tweak it a bit but I got the yips. I'm just medium pace now, up and down the wicket. Few offcutters.

> *He glances at the sofa.*

Do you want me to get in?

TERRY. You can if you take your shoes off.

> DONALD *takes off his shoes and gets under the blanket the opposite way round to* TERRY, *so they're facing each other. There's no sexual tension between them at all.*

DONALD. Do you mind if I ask you something, sir?

TERRY. Ask it.

DONALD. Who's the greatest cricketer that you ever seen?

TERRY. Batsman or bowler?

DONALD. Either.

> TERRY *thinks for a moment.*

TERRY. Well, to see Wally Hammond play an innings at any time in the 1930s was pretty special.

DONALD. I bet it was, sir.

> *Pause.*

TERRY. It made one proud to be English.

Pause.

DONALD. I'm always proud to be English.

Pause.

TERRY. So am I.

The End.